Fortress Europe

By the Editors of Time-Life Books

Alexandria, Virginia

TIME
LIFE ®

Time-Life Books is a division of
Time Life Inc., a wholly owned subsidiary of

The Time Inc. Book Company
Time-Life Books

PRESIDENT: Mary N. Davis

Managing Editor: Thomas H. Flaherty
Director of Editorial Resources:
Elise D. Ritter-Clough
Director of Photography and Research:
John Conrad Weiser
Editorial Board: Dale M. Brown, Roberta Conlan,
Laura Foreman, Lee Hassig, Jim Hicks, Blaine
Marshall, Rita Thievon Mullin, Henry Woodhead
*Assistant Director of Editorial Resources/Training
Manager:* Norma E. Shaw

PUBLISHER: Robert H. Smith

Associate Publisher: Ann M. Mirabito
Editorial Director: Russell B. Adams, Jr.
Marketing Director: Anne C. Everhart
Production Manager: Prudence G. Harris
Supervisor of Quality Control: James King

Editorial Operations
Production: Celia Beattie
Library: Louise D. Forstall
Computer Composition: Deborah G. Tait
(Manager), Monika D. Thayer,
Janet Barnes Syring, Lillian Daniels
Interactive Media Specialist: Patti H. Cass

The Cover: A German sentry stands atop a concrete
bunker housing a powerful coastal gun in northern
France. The emplacement was part of the Atlantic
Wall, the name Adolf Hitler gave to the line of coastal fortifications extending from southern Norway
to the French border with Spain, which he built as
a defensive rampart protecting his west European
conquests from an Allied invasion.

This volume is one of a series that chronicles
the rise and eventual fall of Nazi Germany. Other
books in the series include:
The SS
Fists of Steel
Storming to Power
The New Order
The Reach for Empire
Lightning War
Wolf Packs
Conquest of the Balkans
Afrikakorps
The Center of the Web
Barbarossa
War on the High Seas
The Twisted Dream
The Road to Stalingrad
The Shadow War
The Heel of the Conqueror
The Southern Front
The Apparatus of Death
Scorched Earth

The Third Reich

SERIES EDITOR (Acting): John Newton
Series Administrator: Philip Brandt George
Editorial Staff for *Fortress Europe:*
Senior Art Director: Raymond Ripper
Picture Editor: Jane Jordan
Text Editors: Roberta Conlan, Paul Mathless
Senior Writer: Stephanie A. Lewis
Associate Editors/Research: Katya Sharpe Cooke,
Trudy Pearson (Principals), Oobie Gleysteen
Assistant Art Director: Lorraine D. Rivard
Copy Coordinator: Ann Lee Bruen
Picture Coordinator: Jennifer Iker
Editorial Assistant: Alan Schager

Special Contributors: Ronald H. Bailey,
Charles Clark, Walter Guzzardi, Lydia Preston
Hicks, Charles Phillips, Peter Pocock (text);
Martha Lee Beckington, Ann Louise Gates, Linda
Lee, Kevin A. Mahoney, Danielle S. Pensley,
Marilyn Murphy Terrell (research); Roy Nanovic
(index)

Correspondents: Elisabeth Kraemer-Singh
(Bonn), Christine Hinze (London), Christina
Lieberman (New York), Maria Vincenza Aloisi
(Paris), Ann Natanson (Rome). Valuable
assistance was also provided by: Judy Aspinall
(London), Glenn Mack, Juan Sosa (Moscow),
Elizabeth Brown, Katheryn White (New York).

First printing. Printed in U.S.A.

Published simultaneously in Canada.
School and library distribution by Silver Burdett
Company, Morristown, New Jersey 07960.

TIME-LIFE is a trademark of Time Warner Inc.
U.S.A.

**Library of Congress Cataloging in
Publication Data**

Fortress Europe / by the editors of
Time-Life Books.
    p.   cm. — (The Third Reich)
    Includes bibliographical references and index.
    ISBN 0-8094-7033-0 (trade)
    ISBN 0-8094-7034-9 (lib. bdg.)
    1. World War, 1939-1945—Campaigns—
France. 2. Atlantic Wall (France and Belgium).
3. Germany—History—Bombardment, 1939-
1945. 4. World War, 1939-1945—Aerial operations.
I. Time-Life Books. II. Series.
D761.F67 1992   91-29938
940.54'214—dc20   CIP

Other Publications:

THE NEW FACE OF WAR
HOW THINGS WORK
WINGS OF WAR
CREATIVE EVERYDAY COOKING
COLLECTOR'S LIBRARY OF THE UNKNOWN
CLASSICS OF WORLD WAR II
TIME-LIFE LIBRARY OF CURIOUS AND UNUSUAL FACTS
AMERICAN COUNTRY
VOYAGE THROUGH THE UNIVERSE
THE TIME-LIFE GARDENER'S GUIDE
MYSTERIES OF THE UNKNOWN
TIME FRAME
FIX IT YOURSELF
FITNESS, HEALTH & NUTRITION
SUCCESSFUL PARENTING
HEALTHY HOME COOKING
UNDERSTANDING COMPUTERS
LIBRARY OF NATIONS
THE ENCHANTED WORLD
THE KODAK LIBRARY OF CREATIVE PHOTOGRAPHY
GREAT MEALS IN MINUTES
THE CIVIL WAR
PLANET EARTH
COLLECTOR'S LIBRARY OF THE CIVIL WAR
THE EPIC OF FLIGHT
THE GOOD COOK
WORLD WAR II
HOME REPAIR AND IMPROVEMENT
THE OLD WEST

For information on and a full description of any
of the Time-Life Books series listed above, please
call 1-800-621-7026 or write:
Reader Information
Time-Life Customer Service
P.O. Box C-32068
Richmond, Virginia 23261-2068

General Consultants

Col. John R. Elting, USA (Ret.), former associate professor at West Point, has written
or edited some twenty books, including
*Swords around a Throne, The Superstrate-
gists,* and *American Army Life,* as well as
Battles for Scandinavia in the Time-Life
Books World War II series. He was chief con-
sultant to the Time-Life series The Civil War.

Jon M. Bridgman, Professor of Military History at the University of Washington, spe-
cializes in the WWII period. He is the author
of numerous works on the subject, including
The Revolt of the Hereros and *The End of the
Holocaust: The Liberation of the Camps.*

Contents

A massive German coastal gun protrudes from a bunker under construction in northern France in 1943. Photographs such as this one inspired German public confidence in Hitler's Atlantic Wall: The people were never told that only a few key port areas were so heavily fortified.

Confrontation in the West

Field Marshal Gerd von Rundstedt, commander in chief of the German forces in the west, inspects a section of the Atlantic Wall in the spring of 1944. The veteran general did not believe the wall could prevent a resolute Allied assault and privately referred to it as a "mere showpiece."

eneral Alfred Jodl, chief of operations of the armed forces high command (OKW), delivered a confidential speech to a group of Nazi gauleiters assembled in Munich on November 7, 1943, to celebrate the twentieth anniversary of Adolf Hitler's Beer Hall Putsch. The past several months had been disastrous for Germany, and the general's talk, entitled "The Strategic Position at the Beginning of the Fifth Year of War," detailed the predicament confronting the Reich.

Jodl recited a litany of setbacks: the collapse of Axis forces in North Africa; the Allied invasion of Italy; the overthrow of Benito Mussolini; the Italian armistice; the failed German offensive at Kursk; the Red Army counteroffensive that had reclaimed a large section of the Ukraine; the U-boat failures in the Atlantic; and the Allied air war over Germany, which had brought the worst horrors of the front to the doorstep of nearly every German home.

"Solely through the fault of England," Jodl declared in a curious misplacement of blame, "the war has assumed forms such as were believed to be no longer possible since the days of the racial and religious wars. Up and down the country, the devil of subversion strides. All the cowards are seeking a way out, or—as they call it—a political solution. They say we must negotiate while there is still something in hand." Jodl concluded his gloomy assessment with a prediction—the coming Anglo-American invasion of Europe, he said, "will decide the war."

Although he was no military expert, Nazi propaganda minister Joseph Goebbels also recognized the perils facing the Reich. The man who had once derided the fighting quality of Germany's enemies now was confiding to his diary that "it was not true that British soldiers lacked experience or skill," and he was secretly asking himself how anyone returning from the eastern front could continue to insist on the "absolute superiority of our men over the Red Army—when all we do is retreat and retreat."

Goebbels expressed none of these sentiments publicly. Instead, Hitler's propaganda maven put a positive spin on the Reich's rapidly deteriorating situation by coining a ringing catchword—*Festung Europa*, or Fortress Europe. The concept of a Germany inside a huge citadel was a comforting

The Atlantic Wall on the Eve of Its Fatal Test

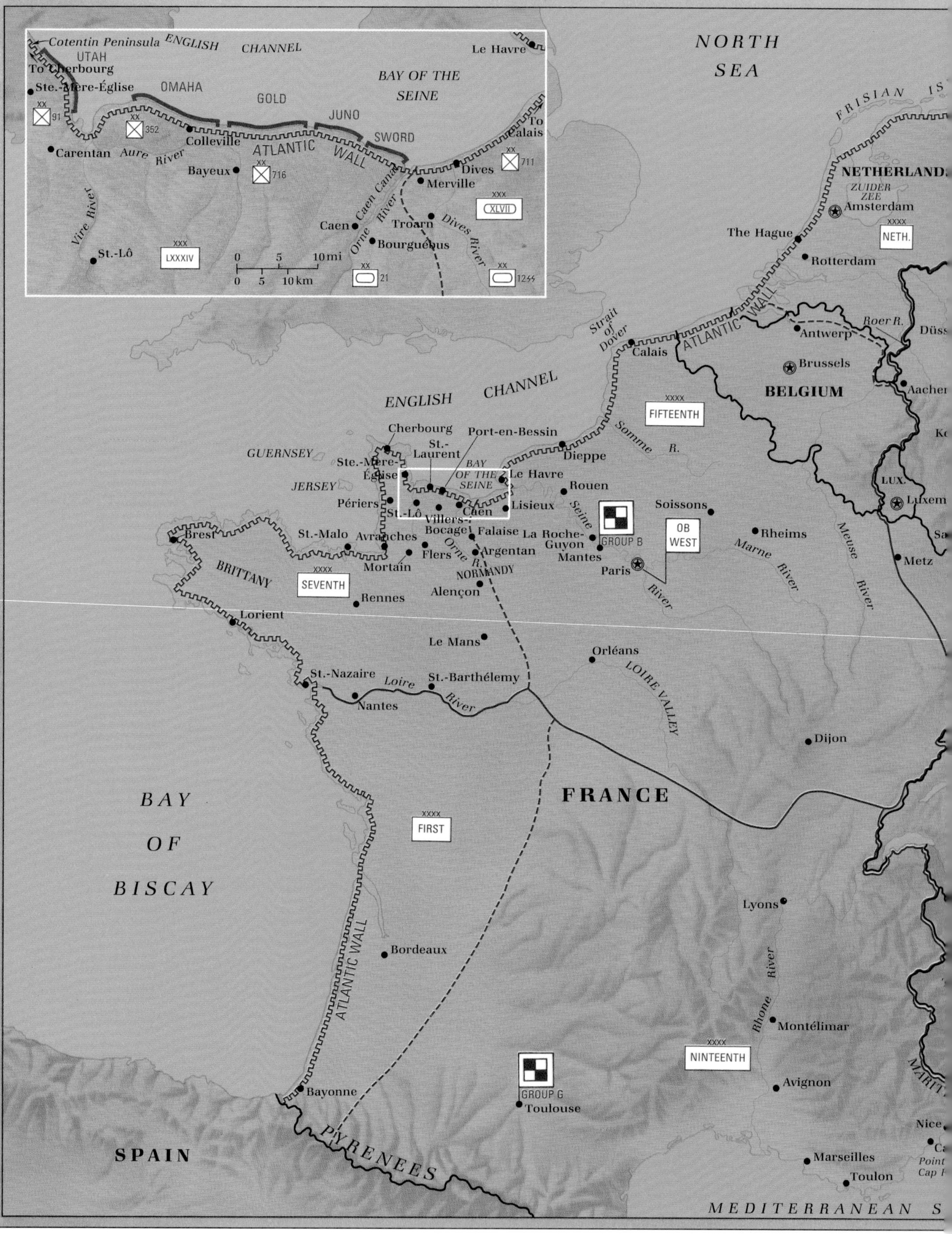

Inset map (upper left)

Cotentin Peninsula

ENGLISH CHANNEL

UTAH

To Cherbourg

Ste.-Mère-Église

OMAHA

Le Havre

BAY OF THE SEINE

GOLD

JUNO

To Calais

91

352

Colleville

SWORD

Carentan

Aure River

ATLANTIC WALL

711

716

Bayeux

Dives

Merville

XLVII

Vire River

Caen Canal

Orne River

Dives River

St.-Lô

Caen

Troarn

Bourguébus

LXXXIV

0   5   10 mi

0   5   10 km

21

1255

Main map

NORTH SEA

FRISIAN IS.

ATLANTIC WALL

NETHERLAND

ZUIDER ZEE

Amsterdam

The Hague

Rotterdam

NETH.

Roer R.

Düss.

Antwerp

Brussels

BELGIUM

Aacher

Strait of Dover

Calais

ATLANTIC WALL

FIFTEENTH

Somme R.

LUX.

Luxem.

ENGLISH CHANNEL

Cherbourg

St.-Laurent

Port-en-Bessin

Dieppe

Rouen

Soissons

Rheims

Meuse River

GUERNSEY

Ste.-Mère-Église

BAY OF THE SEINE

Le Havre

Marne River

Metz

JERSEY

Périers

Lisieux

Seine River

GROUP B

OB WEST

St.-Lô

Villers-Bocage

Caen

Brest

St.-Malo

Avranches

Falaise

La Roche-Guyon

Flers

Orne R.

Argentan

Mantes

Paris

BRITTANY

Mortain

NORMANDY

SEVENTH

Rennes

Alençon

Lorient

Le Mans

Orléans

LOIRE VALLEY

Dijon

St.-Nazaire

Loire River

St.-Barthélemy

Nantes

FRANCE

BAY OF BISCAY

FIRST

Lyons

ATLANTIC WALL

Bordeaux

Rhone River

Montélimar

NINTEENTH

Avignon

Bayonne

GROUP G

Toulouse

Nice

SPAIN

PYRENEES

Marseilles

Point Cap F

Toulon

MEDITERRANEAN S.

8

In the spring of 1944, one million German troops under the command of Field Marshal Gerd von Rundstedt, commander in chief West, girded to defend the Atlantic Wall, the 2,400-mile-long string of coastal fortifications (*crenelated line*) extending from the North Cape in Norway to the French-Spanish border. Adolf Hitler thought the most likely Allied invasion target would be the Pas-de-Calais, the area of France closest to England, and concentrated his most formidable defenses there. When the invasion came on June 6, 1944, however, the Allies picked a sixty-mile-long stretch of the Normandy beach at the Bay of the Seine, an area defended by soldiers from Army Group B, commanded by Field Marshal Erwin Rommel. The American, British, and Canadian assault troops, 170,000 strong, landed at five different sites (*inset*).

notion to a troubled people. Of course, a fortress needed ramparts, so Goebbels spoke glowingly of an East Wall, which stretched in his fertile imagination from Leningrad to the Dnieper River, and of an Atlantic Wall along the coast of western Europe. But even as Goebbels was conjuring up his evocative images, Fortress Europe had begun to crumble. The Red Army had already hurdled the Dnieper, and the Atlantic Wall was only partially complete. And across the English Channel, the British and the Americans were assembling the most powerful amphibious force in all history.

Before the war, Hitler had made brilliant psychological use of another defensive barrier, the West Wall, a band of fortifications facing the French Maginot Line that he constructed to protect Germany's western border while he expanded eastward into Czechoslovakia. The concrete bunkers, pillboxes, and antitank traps helped convince England and France that the strategic map of Europe had changed, aiding Hitler's bluff during the 1938 Munich crisis. But once the war began, there had been no more talk of walls or fortresses. Defensive thinking of any kind was anathema to the Führer, who had designed the Wehrmacht for short, fast, offensive actions. That attitude changed as his ambitions forced Germany into a multifront war.

In the fall of 1940, Hitler, disappointed with the Luftwaffe's failure to defeat the British Royal Air Force (RAF), postponed indefinitely Operation Sea Lion, the planned invasion of England. He decided to first dispose of his ally of convenience and ideological enemy, Communist Russia. Giving little thought to defending his newly conquered lands in the west, Hitler began shifting troops eastward for Operation Barbarossa, the invasion of the Soviet Union. One by one, the three German army groups that had won the battle for France departed, leaving behind only Army Group D, consisting of the First, Seventh, and Sixth (later replaced by the Fifteenth) armies, under Field Marshal Erwin von Witzleben, who received the additional title of commander in chief West.

On June 22, 1941, more than three million German soldiers, supported by 3,300 panzers, 7,000 artillery pieces, and 2,770 planes, crashed across the western border of the Soviet Union. But after stunning early successes, the attack stalled in front of Moscow before a rallying Red Army and the harsh Russian winter. Hitler had reckoned on the rapid collapse of the Soviets. He had been utterly wrong. Blitzkrieg had failed, and now Germany faced a vast new front defended by an aroused and implacable foe. As the war in the east siphoned off more and more troops from occupied Europe, the creation of an Atlantic Wall as a substitute for adequate troop strength in the west became the cornerstone of German strategy.

Until now, the German operations in the western theater had been geared for the attack. The Todt Organization, the huge state public works outfit that had built the autobahn and the West Wall, and had overall responsibility for construction projects in the occupied territories, had begun building U-boat berths in various French ports, including Brest, Lorient, Saint-Nazaire, and Bordeaux, in order to have easier access to Allied shipping targets. The organization also had built several coastal batteries between Calais and Boulogne, along the Strait of Dover, the narrow waist of water that connects the North Sea with the English Channel. The big guns, which were capable of hitting the English coast twenty miles away, had been intended to provide artillery support for Operation Sea Lion. They would soon become the propaganda showpieces of the nascent Atlantic Wall.

The idea of a western bastion was introduced by Field Marshal Wilhelm Keitel, chief of the armed forces high command, in a special directive dated December 14, 1941. "The coastal regions of the Arctic Ocean, North Sea, and Atlantic Ocean controlled by us," he wrote, "are ultimately to be built into a new West Wall in order that we can repel with certainty any landing attempts, even of the strongest enemy forces, with the smallest possible number of permanently assigned field troops."

The Atlantic Wall would not be a true wall, nor even a continuous line of bunkers. Building such a barrier along the entire length of the French, Belgian, Dutch, Danish, and Norwegian coasts—some 2,400 miles not including the French Mediterranean—would have stretched the German construction industry far beyond its capacity. But Hitler was not concerned. As he spelled out in Directive 40, issued on March 23, 1942, the Atlantic Wall would be a comprehensive coastal defense system combining fixed fortifications with mobile forces. Only those sections of the coast that would most likely be attacked would be heavily fortified: They included the large seaports, the U-boat bases, and the important river estuaries.

Serious work began under sixty-seven-year-old Field Marshal Gerd von Rundstedt, who had recently replaced the ailing Field Marshal Witzleben. Witzleben went into retirement. Two years later, he would be executed as one of the principal conspirators in the July 20, 1944, assassination plot against Hitler. Rundstedt, who knew of the plot but played no part in it, had led the main German attack in the victory over France in 1940 and had commanded Army Group South in the Ukraine during Operation Barbarossa until December 1941, when Hitler dismissed him following a disagreement over strategy.

Rundstedt set up his headquarters, or *Oberbefehlshaber,* in Paris. It was known as OB West, the high command in western Europe, and was responsible to Hitler and OKW. Rundstedt began his new assignment by standardizing the various warning procedures and by attempting to raise the number and the quality of his combat troops. In July 1942, he selected the key areas that were to be heavily fortified. In the Netherlands, they consisted of the ports of Den Helder, Ijmuiden, the Hook of Holland, and the town of Vlissingen at the mouth of the Scheldt estuary, and in France, the ports of Dunkirk, Calais, Boulogne, Le Havre, Cherbourg, and Saint-Malo on the Channel coast; and Brest, Lorient, Saint-Nazaire, and La Rochelle on the Atlantic coast. These *Festungsbereiche* (fortress zones) or *Verteidigungsbereiche* (defensive zones), as they were interchangeably called, were designed to resist attacks from land as well as from the sea.

With the United States now at war with Germany, Hitler knew that Allied military strength would grow stronger, and he began to speculate where the Allies might strike first on the Continent. He was determined to avoid a second front. "There is only one battlefront," he boasted. "The other fronts can be defended with only slight strength."

Hitler spelled out his demands for a greatly strengthened Atlantic Wall on August 13, 1942. He wanted 15,000 permanent defensive positions built by the end of spring 1943, to be manned by 300,000 combat troops, supported by a reserve force of 150,000 soldiers. The magnitude of his construction goals stunned the managers of the Todt Organization. They lacked the equipment and the manpower for such an undertaking, even with the addition of tens of thousands of conscripted foreign workers, and estimated that they could accomplish only 40 percent of it by the deadline.

A few days later, on August 19, 1942, the Allies launched an amphibious raid against the French port of Dieppe, located on the English Channel, 100 miles southwest of the Pas-de-Calais section of France. It was a bloody catastrophe for the Allies. The multinational landing force of some 6,000 men suffered 50 percent casualties and was thrown back into the sea. The Allies had attacked exactly the kind of defensive system that Hitler had in mind for the Atlantic Wall, and it had withstood the test with flying colors.

The Dieppe raid intensified Hitler's commitment to fixed fortifications, and by the end of 1942, the Atlantic Wall had become a major component of Germany's war strategy. The Todt Organization's pessimistic estimates, however, proved accurate. When the spring 1943 deadline arrived, construction was not even close to half-finished. Still, some portions of the wall had been completed, especially along the Channel coast and the Pas-de-Calais. The Führer and his general staff thought that this stretch of coastline was the most likely spot for an Allied invasion. Although neither Boulogne nor Calais was a major seaport, they each had the tactical advantage of being closer to Britain than any other harbors on the Continent and the strategic advantage of opening directly into Belgium, which afforded the shortest land route into the Reich.

Costly Rehearsal for a Second Front

While the Germans struggled to piece together an Atlantic Wall strategy in the early part of 1942, the Allies were busy making plans of their own. Convinced that a final victory could not be achieved without establishing a second front, the Allied commanders decided to stage a direct assault on an occupied French harbor. In the process, they hoped to draw German troops away from the beleaguered Soviet Union and engage the Luftwaffe in a decisive air battle.

In the wee hours of August 19, 1942, a fleet of 237 Royal Navy ships steamed across the English Channel bound for an eleven-mile strip of French coastline. The Allied force, which included 5,000 Canadian infantrymen, 1,100 British Commandos, 15 Free French soldiers, and 50 U.S. Rangers, was about to launch one of the biggest raids of the war against the German defenses at Dieppe.

Operation Jubilee, as the mission was called, relied on surprise to carry the day. That hope was dashed, however, when the Allied fleet encountered a small German merchant convoy with an armed escort off the coast of Dieppe. The ensuing skirmish foiled the mission's precise timing; several of the leading assault teams did not land on the beach until after sunrise, in the face of a fully alerted enemy.

From their garrisons atop the high chalk cliffs that shelter Dieppe from the sea, the Germans opened fire on the invaders. After a day of fierce fighting, 1,600 Allied soldiers lay dead or wounded; another 2,000 were taken prisoner. "Dieppe has shown," crowed a Munich newspaper, "that the German rampart on the Atlantic coast is up to all tests."

13

Two wounded Canadians lie on the beach at Dieppe near an abandoned tank, while a landing craft burns on the water. Sixty-five percent of the 5,000-man Canadian force became casualties; Germany lost 591 soldiers killed or wounded.

Lessons Learned from Victory and Defeat

The Dieppe raid proved to be a costly rehearsal for the second front. The Allies failed either to cripple the Luftwaffe or to divert German troops from Russia. But for the planners of the incursion, as Winston Churchill later wrote, the action was "a mine of experience." It taught the Allies the folly of attacking a heavily fortified port and reinforced the need for overwhelming fire support during the initial stages of an assault.

For Hitler, Dieppe was proof that the Allied main invasion would be directed against a similar target. This belief led him to neglect the defense of the open beaches in favor of fortifying the major harbors. He ignored the advice of veteran commander Field Marshal Gerd von Rundstedt, who warned: "It would be an error to believe that the enemy will mount his next operation in the same manner. Next time, he will do things differently."

German soldiers inspect one of twenty-eight Churchill tanks that the Allies left behind. Water-proofed to operate in six feet of water, these new Churchills intrigued the Germans, who brought in experts to analyze the tanks' strengths and weaknesses.

German guards parade members of the Canadian 2d Division through the streets of Dieppe before sending them to prisoner-of-war camps. Hitler rewarded the local citizenry for not help-ing the Allies by awarding the town a gift of 10 million francs and by releasing Dieppe natives from German prison camps.

The Atlantic Wall fortress zones stretched for several miles along a section of coast and consisted of two defensive areas: perimeter fortifications and strongpoints. The perimeter installations, located near the beaches, included antitank ditches, personnel trenches, and embankments. The strongpoints were placed several hundred yards inland and surrounded by barbed-wire entanglements, machine-gun nests, and antitank walls. The center of a typical strongpoint was a bunker with reinforced concrete walls six and a half feet thick, housing a battery of three or four 150-mm or 210-mm artillery pieces. Each strongpoint had its own power source. Some of them were camouflaged to protect against air raids; many others were surrounded by extensive minefields. Nearby were smaller bunkers housing a communications center, ammunition rooms, a decontamination area in case of gas attack, and sleeping quarters for the 80 to 150 men who made up the gun crews. A hospital and a water tank also stood at some distance from the main installation. The entire fortress zone was supported by infantry armed with machine guns, light artillery, mortars, antitank guns, and flamethrowers. In addition, other defenses, such as 88-mm antiaircraft guns, were deployed up and down the shoreline.

The long stretches of coast between the fortress zones, however, were covered only by a series of observation posts and a few bunkers. The coastline from the Loire River at Saint-Nazaire to the French border with

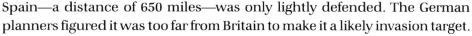

Officials of the Todt Organization, the German public works agency responsible for building the Atlantic Wall, brief their boss, Albert Speer *(center)*, on the progress of construction. Speer took over the organization in 1942 after its founder, Fritz Todt, died in a plane crash. Todt was later honored by having one of the wall's most formidable batteries named after him *(below)*.

Spain—a distance of 650 miles—was only lightly defended. The German planners figured it was too far from Britain to make it a likely invasion target.

As the man responsible for overseeing it all, Field Marshal von Rundstedt was not impressed. He believed that the beach fortifications, no matter how strong, could never do more than temporarily hold up the invaders. To defeat the enemy, a large armored mobile reserve would be necessary to strike the Allied armies after they had landed but before they had consolidated their positions. To close associates, he complained that the wall was nothing but a gigantic bluff, a "propaganda wall."

Rundstedt was less concerned about the unfortified stretches of beach than about the number and quality of his troops and the strength of his reserves—and with good reason. Germany was nearing the limits of its human resources. Ostensibly, OB West had fifty-eight divisions available to guard nearly 2,400 miles of coastline. Hitler, however, had long used Rundstedt's command as a source for making good the mounting losses of troops in the east, and more recently in Italy as well. Divisions that had been chewed up by the Russians or by the Allies came to Rundstedt to be rested, filled with replacements, refitted, and retrained before returning to the battlefronts. Other divisions consisted of inexperienced units in the west that had been sent for advanced training before Hitler shoved them into the heavy fighting in Russia or Italy.

With the exception of a few paratroop and panzer units, all of Rundstedt's coastal divisions were at less than full strength and of inferior quality, made up of men in their late thirties or older, untrained boys, and others deemed unfit for the rigors of the battlefront. Their rolls were supplemented by *Volksdeutsche*, or Ethnic Germans, from all across Europe, and by non-Germans recruited from the occupied territories. Many of the latter were Soviet prisoners of war—Armenians, Azerbaijanis, Ukrainians, Georgians, Tartars, Cossacks, and other ethnic groups—who became "anti-Bolshevik volunteers." Some of them joined the German army to avoid the horrors of the eastern front prisoner-of-war camps. Others had political reasons—they despised Stalin and wanted to rid their homelands of communism.

Joining these motley warriors were a number of German troops transferred from the eastern front because of wounds, frostbite, or sickness. The 70th Infantry Division, for example, consisted almost entirely of soldiers with painful stomach ailments and was called variously the "Whipped

Cream" or "White Bread" Division because of special dietary requirements.

The coastal divisions' weapons and equipment were also second-rate, much of the matériel foreign made and obsolete. There was a severe shortage of tanks, and many units lacked even horse-drawn transport.

In October 1943, Rundstedt expressed his concerns in a pessimistic letter to Hitler, writing that with the troops at his disposal, he could not defend the Atlantic Wall but only ensure that it was covered. His chief of staff, General Günther Blumentritt, described the letter as an "unadorned picture" of the true situation. Hitler responded by issuing Directive 51 on November 3. While the Führer accepted many of Rundstedt's arguments, he still believed that the coastal fortresses could thwart an Allied invasion provided they had enough men, ammunition, and supplies—and firm orders not to withdraw.

The time had come for a fundamental shift in German policy. Since the launching of Operation Barbarossa in June 1941, German energies had been largely devoted to defeating the Russians. "The threat from the east remains," Hitler declared, "but an even greater danger now appears in the west: an Anglo-Saxon landing." Land could always be sacrificed on the vast eastern front, but in the west, where distances were short, the Reich's survival was at stake. "Here," he wrote, "if the enemy succeeds in breaching our defenses along a wide front, consequences of staggering proportions will follow within a short time. All signs point to an offensive against the western front of Europe, at the latest in the spring. For that reason, I can no longer justify the further weakening of the west in favor of other theaters of war. I have, therefore, decided to strengthen the defenses in the west."

Henceforth, Hitler decreed, the greater part of the new heavy weapons production would be sent to the Atlantic Wall. He also ordered the immediate dispatch of eight months' worth of ammunition and supplies to the fortified zones and forbade the transfer of any divisions in the west without his express approval. Hitler echoed Rundstedt in stressing the importance of preparing for a massive armored counterattack against an enemy beachhead. "The problem is," he said, "to make the large number of units available to us into a first-rate, offensively oriented, fully mobile reserve through intensive training." The *Schwerpunkt*, or point of the main defensive effort, would continue to be the Channel coast.

As a reflection of the gravity of the situation, Hitler dispatched Germany's most famous general, the legendary Field Marshal Erwin Rommel, former commander of the Afrikakorps, to assess the coastal defenses. The German high command expected to benefit from Rommel's experience and sound technical knowledge, and also hoped that his presence would calm the German public and worry the Allies.

A German bunker is cleverly painted with imitation beams to resemble the private homes on either side of it. The German engineers followed the dictum that camouflage is as important as thick concrete.

Rommel began his inspection tour in mid-December 1943 amid a blaze of publicity. Joseph Goebbels's Nazi propaganda machine launched a barrage of newspaper articles, radio broadcasts, and newsreels. The Desert Fox played along willingly. He told the photographer who followed him everywhere, "You may do with me what you like, if only it leads to postponing the invasion for a week."

Rommel was dismayed by what he found. He was so shocked by the lack of an overall strategic plan that, at first, he dismissed the whole idea of the Atlantic Wall as a figment of Hitler's imagination, calling it a *Wolkenkuckensheim*, a cloud-cuckoo-land. He rated the army troops he saw as no more than "barely adequate," and he wrote off the navy and the air force as all but useless. The Luftwaffe could muster no more than 300 serviceable fighter planes to meet the thousands of British and American aircraft that could be expected to cover the skies over the invasion beaches, and the navy had only a handful of ships, none larger than a destroyer.

Given the manifest weakness of the German forces, Rommel could see no alternative except to make every effort to stop the invaders at the water's edge. From his experience in North Africa, he was convinced that Allied fighter planes and bombers would preclude any large-scale movement of German troops hoping to counterattack against an established beachhead. As Rommel graphically put it: "Anyone who has to fight, even with the most modern weapons, against an enemy in complete control of the air, fights like a savage against modern European troops." The problem was that Rommel had no authority to implement his recommendations. He could only hope that Hitler and OKW would pass them along to Rundstedt with orders to carry them out.

Rundstedt, for his part, respected Rommel's leadership abilities but resented having a junior officer sent to inspect his defenses. As Rommel established his headquarters in Fontainebleau some sixty-five miles south of Paris, Rundstedt complained bitterly to OKW in Berlin, bluntly asking Field Marshal Keitel if Rommel was being groomed as his successor. Keitel's assurances scarcely mollified him. Rundstedt was already thoroughly disenchanted with the chain of command within OB West.

Rundstedt controlled neither the Luftwaffe nor the navy. He could request air or antiaircraft support from Field Marshal Hugo Sperrle, the commander of the 3d Air Fleet, but Sperrle took his orders directly from Luftwaffe chief Hermann Göring and would often simply ignore Rundstedt's requests. The commander of Naval Group West, Admiral Theodor Krancke, answered directly to Grand Admiral Karl Dönitz not only for sea operations but also for harbor defenses. The Waffen-SS divisions, while under army command, could appeal to Reichsführer-SS Heinrich Himmler if they did not like their orders. And the Todt Organization worked directly for armaments minister Albert Speer. Rundstedt could not even move his own units without Hitler's permission. In a remark made after the war, Rundstedt vented his disgust with this state of affairs: "As commander in chief West," he said with biting sarcasm, "my sole prerogative was to change the guard in front of my gate."

Hitler decided the matter of Rommel's official status by making him commander of Army Group B, under Rundstedt. Army Group B was responsible for defending the coast from the tip of Holland to the Loire estuary. It consisted of the occupation army in the Netherlands under Luftwaffe General Friedrich Christiansen; the Fifteenth Army under General Hans von Salmuth, stationed between the Scheldt estuary in Belgium and the Dives River at the Bay of the Seine in Normandy; and the Seventh Army under General Friedrich Dollmann, which guarded the Cotentin Peninsula, the Calvados coast in Normandy, and Brittany. The remainder of Rundstedt's command, the First Army under Lieut. General Kurt von der Chevallerie along the Bay of Biscay and the Nineteenth Army under General Georg von Sodenstern along the French Mediterranean, became Army Group G, led by General Johannes Blaskowitz.

Rommel's authority over the Seventh and Fifteenth armies extended only six miles inland, and at first, there was not a single panzer division in his command. Rundstedt had consolidated the nine tank divisions in northern France into Panzer Group West under the command of General Leo Geyr von Schweppenburg. Geyr had been schooled in fighting the Russians, and he subscribed to Rundstedt's conviction that an Allied invasion force could be stopped only by a crushing blow from massed armor after it had landed. Geyr insisted on concentrating Panzer Group West away from the endangered beaches. Rommel protested vigorously to Rundstedt, whose only concession was to order Geyr to place his armored divisions closer to the coast. Irritated, Rommel remarked to his former chief of staff in North Africa and commander of the Panzer Lehr Division, Lieut. General Fritz Bayerlein: "Our friends from the east cannot imagine what they are in for."

The debate over strategy eventually reached Hitler. In principle, the Führer sided with Rommel. The fundamental logic of the Atlantic Wall, after all, was to stop the invasion before it reached the shore. But because no one knew where the British and Americans might attack, the Führer hesitated to countermand Rundstedt's plan, which offered the apparent advantage of holding the panzer divisions in readiness to respond wherever events dictated. The disagreement was never resolved, and when the Allies finally came, it would contribute hugely to their success.

Rommel did have a free hand in improving the coastal defenses in his sector, however, and he set about it with a will. Soon, the beaches of Normandy bristled with a spectacular assortment of antitank and antilanding craft obstacles, many of which Rommel designed himself. To hamper landings by enemy paratroopers and gliders, he ordered some of the farmland behind the beaches flooded. Other areas he laced with ten-foot-high stakes armed with captured shells and connected by wire to detonate the explosives. The troops called them "Rommel's asparagus." Rommel also began a massive mine-laying program to form what he called a "zone of death" extending five to six miles inland from the beaches. Despite monumental supply and transport difficulties, Rommel managed to have some four million mines laid as against fewer than two million laid during the previous three years.

In contrast to the aristocratic Rundstedt with his aloof old-school manners, Rommel was blunt, demanding, and energetic. To implement his tactical conception, he drove himself and his staff relentlessly. He was constantly among the troops and construction battalions, energizing them with his enthusiasm. From out of nowhere, his car would come screeching to a halt, and he would leap out and begin asking questions, pinpointing improper or laggard work on the defenses. "He was an unconventional soldier and very interested in technical things," recalled his naval adviser, Admiral Friedrich Ruge. "He saw the point of any device of a technical kind very quickly. If one gave him an idea in the evening, he would often telephone in the morning and suggest an improvement. He had a strong mechanical bent, and his suggestions were always sound."

Until mid-March 1944, Hitler held firm in his belief that the invaders would come by the short sea route to Calais. The Allies did everything they could to encourage this misconception. In an exercise called Operation Fortitude, they engaged in an elaborate ruse to make the Germans think Lieut. General George S. Patton and a "First U.S. Army Group" were poised in Kent for an attack across the Strait of Dover. Patton had been ostentatiously recalled to Britain from the Mediterranean and given command of the phantom army group. Fake radio traffic, dummy encampments, flotillas of imitation landing craft, false reports sent back by captured German spies—all buttressed the conviction of Hitler and the high command that wherever else the enemy might show up, the main invasion would come in the Pas-de-Calais. Meanwhile, the huge buildup of the real invasion forces went largely unnoticed.

On March 20, Hitler changed his mind. Perhaps German intelligence had got wind of the massive Allied deployment in southern England. Perhaps something in the pattern of Allied bombing triggered his suspicions. For whatever reason, he concluded that the invasion would come on the beaches of Normandy or Brittany. More important, he resolved (for the moment) the great strategic debate between Rundstedt and Rommel by accepting Rommel's view that the invaders would have to be defeated at the water's edge. "The enemy's entire landing operation," he said in a speech that day to the top commanders in the west, "must under no circumstances be allowed to last longer than a matter of hours, or, at the most, days, with the Dieppe attempt as a model."

A volunteer unit, composed of former Indian prisoners of war captured in North Africa and members of a militant Indian nationalist group, snaps to attention for Field Marshal Erwin Rommel. These soldiers were among some 75,000 foreign troops used by the German army to plug manpower gaps in the Atlantic Wall.

Encouraged by the speech, Rommel met with Hitler to request that Geyr's armored reserves be moved up closer to the coast and placed under his direct command. The next day, Hitler agreed. But twenty-four hours later, after protests by Rundstedt and the OKW chief of operations, General Jodl, he reversed his decision. When informed, Rommel was furious and snapped, "The last person out of his door is always right!"

At the beginning of May, Hitler changed his mind again. He still believed that the enemy would land on the beaches of Normandy—and perhaps elsewhere—but that these would be diversionary attacks meant to draw strength from the main invasion in the Pas-de-Calais. Such became the new gospel. Even Rommel, at least at first, agreed with Hitler, although indications are that he later changed his mind and settled on Normandy as the most likely site for the actual invasion. Of all the guesses Hitler made, this one would prove the most costly. When D-day came—and for critical weeks afterward—he would steadfastly refuse to shift the formidable defensive power of the Fifteenth Army to Normandy where it was really needed.

Hitler's final word on the deployment of the armored reserves grew directly from his new opinion about the invasion site. As the debate over the deployment of the panzer divisions continued on into May, Rundstedt refused to intervene, letting his subordinates, Rommel and Geyr, fight it out between themselves. After Geyr traveled to Berchtesgaden for a showdown, the Führer made a compromise that satisfied no one. He let Rommel have his long sought after armored reserve but gave him only part of what he had asked for—and not the best part. Three of the six panzer divisions in northern France—the 2d, the 21st, and the 116th—joined Rommel's Army Group B. Only the 21st Panzer Division, however, was moved close to the Normandy coast, at Caen. The others were stationed east of the Seine River, away from the beaches. The remaining three panzer divisions—the crack 1st SS Panzer, the 12th SS Panzer, and Panzer Lehr—were reassigned as an OKW reserve and could not be moved except by direct order from Hitler. The 12th SS Panzer and Panzer Lehr were sent fifty miles inland, and the 1st SS Panzer was dispatched to Belgium. Having placed fatal restraints on the two men most responsible for defending the Atlantic Wall, the Führer ensured that neither of their strategies could be followed.

On Tuesday, June 6, 1944, the Allies began Operation Overlord, their assault on Fortress Europe, coming ashore on a sixty-mile stretch of Normandy coast on the Bay of the Seine between the Contentin Peninsula and the Orne River. The Germans were caught completely by surprise.

In part, the Germans were fooled by the weather. Because the Luftwaffe's losses had rendered it nearly impotent in the west, German intelligence was able to conduct little aerial reconnaissance. To predict Allied moves, the Germans had to rely to a dangerous extent on informed guesswork. One of their assumptions was that the Allies could not attack in rough seas or without air cover, and that meant they needed good weather.

For most of the week of June 4, the Wehrmacht's weather service predicted foul conditions—overcast skies, high winds, and rain. Admiral Krancke canceled sea patrols on the night of June 5, and onshore, the entire defense force from headquarters to bunker stood down from alert status. General Dollmann, commander of the Seventh Army in Normandy and Brittany, took advantage of the stand-down by ordering his senior officers to Rennes for a map exercise. Rommel had left for Germany at the beginning of the week. He planned to catch some much-needed rest at his home in Herrlingen and celebrate his wife's fiftieth birthday on June 6. Then he planned to go on to Berchtesgaden to consult with Hitler. He left his chief of staff, General Hans Speidel, in charge of Army Group B.

The week of June 4, however, was one of the few periods when, by German calculations, the timing of tide and first light would be favorable for a landing. Gestapo agents who had penetrated the French Resistance warned that an invasion was imminent, and on June 4, Lieut. Colonel Helmut Meyer, a Fifteenth Army intelligence officer, intercepted a coded radio signal to the Resistance indicating that the invasion would begin within forty-eight hours. When this stunning news was forwarded to OKW, OB West, and Army Group B, it evoked no response. Jodl left the matter to Rundstedt, who in turn took it for granted that Rommel's army group would order an alert. With Rommel gone, General Speidel dismissed the message as another rumor.

General Dwight D. Eisenhower, the supreme allied commander, had already called off the invasion once that week because of bad weather. But the Allies enjoyed more accurate weather forecasting than the Germans, thanks to a network of meteorological stations stretching from Nova Scotia to Scotland. The forecasters predicted a break in the foul conditions for several hours on June 6. With tens of thousands of Allied troops crammed into transports and landing craft in the stormy chop off the overcrowded harbors of the English southern coast, Eisenhower made an agonizing last-minute decision to proceed with the attack. It would be led by British Field Marshal Sir Bernard Law Montgomery.

Allied planes carrying one British and two American airborne divisions took off before midnight on June 5, and the invasion fleet steamed out into the Channel. The armada of 1,200 warships, plus some 4,200 landing craft, would deliver two British, one Canadian, and three American infantry divisions to five locations on the Normandy coast early the next morning, while 11,500 planes provided air support.

The Third Reich

BOOKMARK AND MAP KEY

These map symbols, based on those German and Allied staffs used during World War II, show locations of headquarters, sizes of units, branches of service, and names or numbers of units.

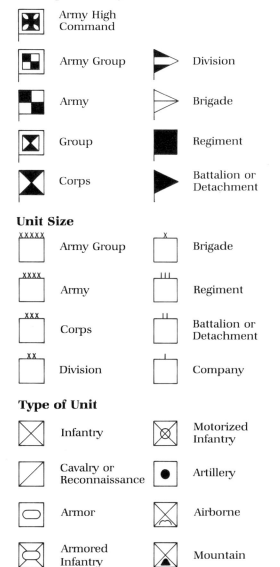

Headquarters Symbols

✠	Army High Command		
◼	Army Group	⬗	Division
◼	Army	▷	Brigade
⊠	Group	◼	Regiment
◤◥	Corps	▶	Battalion or Detachment

Unit Size

XXXXX	Army Group	X	Brigade
XXXX	Army	⫫	Regiment
XXX	Corps	⫪	Battalion or Detachment
XX	Division	I	Company

Type of Unit

⊠	Infantry	⊗	Motorized Infantry
⟋	Cavalry or Reconnaissance	•	Artillery
⊖	Armor	⊠	Airborne
⧖	Armored Infantry	◸	Mountain

Field Fortifications /\/\/\/\/\/\/\

Prepared Defenses ⎍⎍⎍⎍⎍⎍

...tegic objective for the American landing force, led by Lieut. ... N. Bradley of the U.S. First Army, was the port city of ...e tip of the Cotentin Peninsula. The two American airborne ...101st and 82d, were to drop behind the German coastal ... the eastern side of the peninsula, capture key road junc- ...oy bridges over which German reinforcements might come. ...en await the arrival of the U.S. VII Corps, which would form ... flank after it landed at 6:30 a.m. on the section of shoreline ...tah Beach, on the peninsula's east coast. After relieving the ...he VII Corps would build up its forces and then cut off the ...insula and take Cherbourg. Meanwhile, the U.S. V Corps ... the next zone to the east, code-named Omaha Beach. The ...ops were to drive inland and link up with VII Corps on their ... the British XXX Corps on their left.

...ter the American landings, an Anglo-Canadian force com- ...neral Sir Miles C. Dempsey was to land on three adjacent ...itish XXX Corps on Gold Beach, in the center of the Allied ...e British I Corps on Juno Beach and Sword Beach, on the ... Dempsey's objective was to capture Caen, astride the Orne River, and Bayeux, on the main highway between Caen and Cherbourg.

Shortly after midnight, panzergrenadier units east of Montebourg reported that they were engaged with paratroopers identified as members

of the U.S. 82d Airborne Division. A little later, the headquarters of the German 709th Division reported the capture of troops from the U.S. 101st Airborne. At about the same time, Major General Wilhelm Richter, commander of the 716th Infantry Division, called General Erich Marcks, commander of LXXXIV Corps, in what would be the heart of the invasion zone, with information that British paratroopers were landing east of the Orne. Knowing that three enemy airborne divisions had been identified and that landings were taking place in two areas fifty miles apart, Marcks had no doubt that the invasion was on.

Supplies earmarked for the U.S. 82d Airborne Division float down into a field outside of Sainte-Mère-Église on June 7, 1944. The gliders in the foreground had been wrecked the day before during the D-day attack.

At 2:00 a.m., General Marcks put his corps and the 21st Panzer Division on alert and informed Major General Max Pemsel, who was in charge of the Seventh Army in General Dollmann's absence. Pemsel, in turn, called Army Group B headquarters to tell General Speidel, who disagreed that the invasion was in progress. Speidel proved just as stubborn when General Salmuth, the commander of the Fifteenth Army, called a few minutes later to inform him that General Josef Reichert at the 711th Division headquarters had reported the sound of machine-gun fire.

For eight hours, Speidel put off contacting Rommel. Finally, at 10:15 a.m., he called. Rommel took the phone, listened for a moment, and muttered, "How stupid of me." He told Speidel he would cancel his appointment with Hitler and start back immediately. By early afternoon, he was racing across France in his staff car.

A similar misperception occurred at both OB West and OKW. In the predawn hours, Rundstedt, after failing to get through to Jodl at OKW and in spite of his own doubts, on his own authority ordered the 12th SS Panzer and Panzer Lehr divisions to move to the battle area. When Jodl awoke at 6:00 a.m. and was informed by his aides of Rundstedt's actions, he countermanded the order, claiming it was too early to tell whether or not the reports of enemy paratroopers signified the main landing. He refused to disturb the Führer's rest. Hitler, who had long suffered from insomnia, was in a drugged sleep, and no one at OKW was willing to wake him. Not until 10:00 a.m., after the Allies had announced their landing to the world, did Jodl order General Rudolf Schmundt, Hitler's chief adjutant, to rouse the Führer and inform him. Hitler took the news calmly and told Schmundt to have Keitel and Jodl report to him at once. When they arrived, the Führer asked: "Well, is it the invasion or not?" After they gave him a full briefing on the morning's events, Hitler walked to a map of France on the wall and chuckled with amusement. "So, we're off!" he declared.

Much of the German doubt and confusion was the work of the Allied deception plan, Operation Fortitude. Allied planes dropped rubber dummies dressed as paratroopers and rigged with noisemaking devices that simulated machine-gun fire to sow panic behind the beaches. Fortitude personnel filled the airwaves around the Pas-de-Calais with fake radio traffic, dispatched boats towing balloons that showed up on German radar as a gigantic invasion armada heading for Calais, and dropped shredded aluminum foil from planes to give the impression on radar that fleets of bombers and paratroop transports were approaching.

While the Germans dithered, the U.S. 82d and 101st Airborne near Carentan and the British 6th Airborne on the Orne River were struggling to carry out their missions. The British paratroopers had dropped right on target near the Orne and the Caen Canal bridges and the town of Bénouville. Within minutes, they had blown up the assigned bridges—even though most of one brigade had landed in an area Rommel had recently flooded, drowning a number of them. The other British objectives were the coastal battery at Merville, which was in perfect position to shell Sword Beach, and the bridges over the Dives River at Troarn, which the Germans would have to use if they wanted to counterattack the beachheads from the west. After heavy fighting, the British overcame the Merville battery around 5:00 a.m. They destroyed the Dives bridges twenty minutes later.

The American paratroopers were not so fortunate. Low-lying clouds prevented an accurate approach by the glider transports carrying the U.S. 101st Airborne Division, and heavy German antiaircraft fire broke up their formations. The division suffered 30 percent casualties and lost nearly three-quarters of its equipment in the landing. Although scarcely one-third of the 6,600 paratroopers assembled, they succeeded in securing and holding the inland routes to Utah Beach on D-day.

The U.S. 82d Airborne fared even worse. Their landing zones had been poorly marked by the Pathfinders, and the pilots of their transports had to zigzag to dodge the German flak. As a result, the paratroopers landed far from their targets and were dispersed over many miles. Some men drowned in the flooded fields. Most of the others came down in the midst of the German 91st Air Landing Division, which cut them to pieces. The only major objective the 82d Airborne achieved, however, turned out to be immensely important. One of the American units captured Sainte-Mère-Église, effectively shielding Utah Beach from German counterattacks.

Throughout the predawn hours of D-day, the powerful Allied air forces were at work, destroying German airfields, supply depots, and bridges. The bombing dealt an especially heavy blow to German telephone communications, which had already been disrupted by the French Resistance. British and American fighter-bombers knocked out dozens of railroad and highway bridges between Paris and the coast and pummeled the rear area of the German LXXXIV Corps. Then, as the sun came up and the clouds dispersed, they dropped 12,000 tons of bombs on Rommel's coastal fortifications in the invasion zone.

As dawn broke, the men of the German 716th and 352d Infantry divisions stared anxiously out to sea from their bunkers and pillboxes along the Normandy coast. Throughout the night, they had listened to the reports that had been coming into OB West and Army Group B, and they had been on alert since 2:00 a.m. The 352d Infantry Division was a tough outfit, formed six months previously out of eastern front veterans. Although Rommel had moved it into the invasion sector from Saint-Lô several

At a midday briefing on D-day, Luftwaffe chief Hermann Göring shows Hitler one of the Allied landing sites on a map of the Normandy coast. The Führer, who had been conferring with Premier Döme Sztójay of Hungary (*seated, far left*) and Foreign Minister Joachim von Ribbentrop (*top left*), refused to accept the full scope of the invasion: He still believed that the main attack would take place at the Pas-de-Calais.

months earlier, its presence was not known to Allied intelligence agents.

Lance Corporal Hein Severloh, a forward artillery observer, borrowed a pair of binoculars from his battery commander, Lieutenant Frerking. Severloh shared a nearby farmhouse with Frerking and a Sergeant Krone. When the warning alarm sounded, they had rushed down to the dunes of Colleville to join their comrades. As Severloh peered over the concrete parapet through the hazy morning air, Krone asked, "See anything, Hein?"

"Nothing's happening," he said. "Not a thing."

Then, they heard the drone of bombers above the clouds. A succession of blasts shook the earth, the noise tearing at their nerves. But it was over in a few minutes. Somehow, the bombs had missed them—missed the entire battery, as a quick telephone call confirmed. They had no way of knowing that the Allied command, worried about the accuracy of its heavy bombers when flying blind through thick cloud cover, had ordered the drop delayed for a crucial few seconds at the last moment to avoid hitting the approaching invasion fleet. Most of the bombs had fallen harmlessly into the fields behind their bunkers.

The men relaxed, lit cigarettes, and began to prepare breakfast. Lieutenant Frerking came out of the bunker and casually raised his binoculars. What he saw out in the bay transfixed him. "But that's not possible, that's not possible," he gasped. Shoving the glasses into his lance corporal's hands, he rushed back into the bunker. And now Severloh saw it, too—a sight to make the blood run cold: ships, stretching across the horizon in one huge, rolling, unending line; battleships, cruisers, destroyers, command ships, creating a jumble of turrets, antennas, funnels, tethered barrage balloons; and behind them, convoys of troop-filled transports and landing ships, low and awkward in the water—a fleet the size of a city,

Exposed by the low tide, Rommel's offshore obstacles provide the only available cover for the first wave of Americans attacking Omaha Beach. Deadly fire from the German 352d Infantry Division kept the Americans pinned down for six hours and inflicted 2,000 casualties, including the dead GI lying in the sand at right.

headed right for them.

"The big one is coming ashore," shouted Severloh. "Landing craft on our left, off Vierville, making for the beach." Krone joined him. "They must be crazy. Are they going to swim ashore? Right in front of our muzzles?"

The American ships unloaded thirty-two amphibious Sherman tanks, most of which swamped in the deep, choppy water and sank like stones. The few that made it to shore were quickly destroyed by German antitank guns. The first wave of landing craft followed the Shermans. Two of the six craft were sunk by antitank fire. Machine-gun rounds clinking against their metal sides, the four remaining boats reached the first sand bar and dropped their ramps. Stepping off in chest-high water, soldiers of the U.S. 1st Infantry Division, which was spearheading the assault, were cut down by machine-gun fire as they struggled to reach the shore. Within minutes, the Germans had killed so many Americans that the survivors lay hugging the sand, unable or unwilling to move, most of their officers dead or wounded. The slaughter on Omaha Beach had begun.

For almost three hours, the lopsided battle raged. The Germans hit the American artillery units particularly hard, sinking or destroying virtually all of their guns and killing their crews. On the right, the commander of an Allied landing craft, aware of the fate of the first batch of tanks, defied his orders, running his boat all the way into shore to discharge sixteen more Shermans. German antitank fire destroyed or crippled half of them, leaving a total of eight American tanks in fighting condition on all of Omaha Beach.

By midmorning, more than 1,000 Americans lay dead or wounded in the sand. General Bradley realized that the U.S. V Corps was in danger of losing the battle. He called for naval guns to open up, even at the risk of hitting his own troops. Battleships and destroyers trained their guns on the bunkers above Omaha Beach and opened fire. Just as the two German divisions defending the beach were feeling the full might of American

firepower, their own artillery outfits began to run out of ammunition.

The Americans, faced with the choice of remaining behind the skimpy cover of Rommel's offshore obstacles or advancing into the murderous fire, started slowly to move inland. By late morning, small groups, no bigger than squads, broke through the outermost crust of the German defenses.

Strongpoint WN-62 was the first to fall. Hein Severloh's battery had been reduced by then to firing single rounds. The Allied air forces had ensured that not a single bullet was resupplied to the German front line that morning. Severloh himself had fired 12,000 machine-gun rounds at the Americans, and all he had left were tracers. When everyone in his battery had run out of ammunition, they noticed that the surrounding bunkers in the strongpoint had all fallen silent. Now, the bunker was taking direct hits from tank guns and naval fire; it was time to flee. As the crew made a run up the hill behind the battery, the Americans opened fire. Only Severloh and one signalman made it to safety.

Twenty miles to the west, at Utah Beach, the situation was reversed, and the Germans were the ones being slaughtered. In the 709th Infantry Division's Strongpoint W-5, Lieutenant Arthur Jahnke looked out through the smoke and dust thrown up by the Allied naval bombardment. The shelling, following an attack by hundreds of medium bombers, had destroyed all of the strongpoint's antitank guns and many of its bunkers. The men in

Jahnke's bunker lay cringing amid the falling shells and bombs, their hands over their ears. As the tumult died down, a mess orderly cried, "Everything's wrecked! Everything's wrecked! We've got to surrender." Jahnke, a twenty-three-year-old veteran of the Russian front, resisted the panic in the bunker, but in a moment was greeted with the terrifying sight of enemy tanks rising up out of the sea.

Jahnke called the 901st Artillery Regiment for help, but the regiment's guns had been knocked out by the Allied bombardment. He sent a messenger over to the 1261st Artillery Regiment, but the runner was shot by a strafing American fighter plane. Jahnke rallied his men and prepared to defend his sector with a single 88-mm gun, an old French tank turret dug into the sand, and a few machine guns. The gun, damaged by the bombing, jammed after firing one round. The tank turret fired a few bursts from its

Under Canadian guard, troops from the German 716th Infantry Division march off Juno Beach into captivity. By late evening on D-day, the Canadians had secured the beachhead and begun advancing inland toward Douvres and Caen.

machine guns before it was destroyed by a shell from a Sherman tank. Another shell hit the bunker, burying Jahnke in sand. He awoke staring up at the muzzle of an American rifle.

Such was the story everywhere on Utah Beach. The U.S. 4th Infantry Division, led by Brigadier General Theodore Roosevelt, Jr., son of the former American president and famous Rough Rider, spearheaded the attack. The division, swept some 1,500 yards beyond its designated landing zone by the strong Channel current, had come ashore where the underwater obstacles, mines, and gun emplacements were skimpy. The VII Corps took the beach within a few hours, suffering no more than 200 casualties. At noon, it kept its rendezvous with the 101st Airborne inland from the beachhead.

At almost that same time, Lieut. General Karl-Wilhelm von Schlieben, in charge of the defenses on the Cotentin Peninsula, was on his way back to Cherbourg from General Dollmann's ill-timed map exercise in Rennes. Earlier in the day, Schlieben had been ordered by Dollmann to drive to Utah Beach to reinforce the defenders. But Schlieben did not have sufficient

Lieut. Colonel Josef "Pips" Priller, one of the Luftwaffe's premier aces, is helped from his Focke Wulf 190 fighter after flying a sortie on D-day. His plane was one of about 300 German fighters available to fly against the 5,000 Allied fighters that swarmed over the invasion sites.

troops. The 91st Air Landing Division had no leadership. Its commander, General Wilhelm Falley, had been killed during the night in a chance encounter with American paratroopers. And when two regiments of the landing division troops did move up, they were harassed by ambushes, set up by scattered bands of lost American paratroopers, and found the way to the beach blocked by units from the U.S. 82d Airborne Division holding the town of Sainte-Mère-Église. In addition, the continual Allied aerial bombardment made movement of any kind nearly impossible. By dark, the German line behind Utah had collapsed. The Americans had secured a grip on the Cotentin Peninsula that could not be broken.

Meanwhile, the British and the Canadians were also faring well. Knowing he would be up against his old adversary Rommel, Field Marshal Montgomery had insisted on deploying far more tanks in the first waves landing at the three Anglo-Canadian beaches than the Americans had used at Omaha or Utah. He was also more willing to use tanks that had been altered by British technical experts. These tanks had amphibious, minesweeping, and flamethrowing capabilities to meet the special needs of the invasion.

General Wilhelm Richter's 716th Infantry Division held the twenty-one-mile-long stretch of coast known to the Allies as Gold Beach. Not only was his division stretched thin, but one unit, the 441st Ost Battalion, consisted of Soviet former prisoners of war who either fled or surrendered without a fight, opening a yawning gap in the German defense line. Hit hard by the early morning Allied air and naval bombardment, the German coastal forces simply could not stop the landing. By 8:00 a.m., the British 50th Infantry Division had smashed through the fortifications on Gold Beach and proceeded to advance inland.

Matters did not go so smoothly to the east of Gold Beach, where the Canadian 3d Division landing at Juno Beach and the British 3d Division landing at Sword Beach met stiff opposition. Nevertheless, by nightfall both beaches were in Allied hands. The Canadians had broken through the Juno Beach defenses and reached the Caen-Bayeux highway, while the British had fought their way off Sword Beach and made contact with the British 6th Airborne Division across the Orne River on its left flank.

But the rapid Anglo-Canadian advance soon backfired. Montgomery had promised not only to take Caen but also to drive well past it before D-day was out. As the German troops retreated, the British and Canadians rushed headlong toward their goal, paying little attention to the fact that not many of Richter's men were surrendering. A number of them were veterans of the fighting in Russia, where it was common practice for an overmatched unit to fall away, hide until the enemy had passed, and then attack from the rear. The Germans used the same tactic here. At Saint-Croix, behind Juno Beach,

Riding a self-propelled gun camouflaged with shrubbery to hide it from Allied aircraft, members of the 12th SS Panzer Division head toward the battle zone on June 6, 1944. Their unit did not receive marching orders until 4:00 p.m. that day—too late to hinder the landing.

they fought so tenaciously that the Canadians had to backtrack with tanks to retake ground they thought they had won. The British and the Canadians spent so much time repelling unexpected German counterattacks that they could manage to advance only halfway to Caen.

Throughout the day, as the German soldiers up and down the coast fought desperately to prevent a lodgment by the Allies, they cursed the Luftwaffe for not showing up, and they asked each other, "Where are the tanks?" The weakened Luftwaffe did manage to launch a number of sorties, and a few pilots flew with incredible bravery, but they made no difference in the outcome of the battle. The tanks were another matter entirely. Hitler delayed for several hours the release of Rundstedt's armor from the OKW reserves. These panzer divisions, deployed between 50 to 150 miles from the front, were unable to reach the coast due to the relentless Allied bombing—just as Rommel had predicted.

Had Rommel's own armored reserve, the 21st Panzer, reached the beaches quickly, it might have had a substantial impact on the invasion. Instead, it was not until four o'clock in the afternoon that the Germans launched their first armored counterattack. As early as 2:00 a.m., General Richter of the 716th Infantry Division had asked Lieut. General Edgar Feuchtinger, commander of the 21st Panzer Division, to help deal with the paratroopers of the British 6th Airborne Division. It was not until 8:00 a.m. that panzers began moving to the beaches, and by then, the British paratroopers were far less a threat than the Anglo-Canadian invasion force. Frustrated by British control of the only bridge over the Orne north of Caen, then blocked from proceeding through the city by wreckage-strewn streets, the tanks had to make a long detour and took a terrible beating from Allied fighter-bombers before they finally reached the combat zone in midafternoon.

At that point, General Marcks stepped in. He had conferred with OKW and now informed the uncooperative Feuchtinger that the 21st Panzer Division had officially been made part of the LXXXIV Corps. Marcks ordered one company to contain the airborne bridgehead and sent the rest to join the counterattack west of Caen. On the way, the tanks passed Richter. "My troops are lost," he said in anguish. "My whole division is finished."

The two tank battalions that finally pulled into position before the British were a far cry from the magnificent panzers Rommel had wielded in North Africa. One battalion consisted of forty Panzer IVs equipped with older-model, short-barreled guns of limited range. The other battalion was even weaker—sixty obsolete tanks from the arsenals of countries occupied by the Germans. In the ensuing battle, six of the 2d Battalion's Panzer IVs were knocked out in fifteen minutes, before they could even get within range of the British. The 1st Battalion quickly lost ten of its motley retinue of tanks.

While the tank battalions were being pounded, General Marcks led the 21st Panzer Division's 192d Panzergrenadier Regiment in an attempt to drive a wedge between British positions on the beach, hoping to follow up with enough troops to attack the Allied flanks on either side and roll them up. The regiment's 1st Battalion struck exactly between Sword and Juno beaches and penetrated to the coast at 8:00 p.m. Marcks wanted to reinforce the unit, but just then, a huge British glider airlift—planned much earlier and having nothing to do with the German move—swooped low overhead and frightened Feuchtinger into believing it was an attempt to cut off the tanks. He ordered an immediate withdrawal, and Germany's only armored counterattack on D-day was over.

Looking back on the historic day years later, one of Rundstedt's operations officers ruefully said: "It is a matter of irony that Eisenhower, the servant of the great democracies, was given full powers of command over an armed force consisting of all three services. With us, living under a dictatorship where unity of command might have been taken for granted, each of the services fought its own battle." ✚

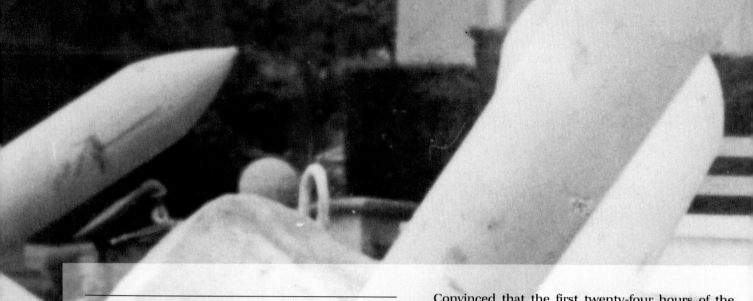

Blueprint for a "Zone of Death"

When Field Marshal Erwin Rommel took command of the German defenses along the Channel coast in January 1944, he set about turning the Atlantic Wall into a real obstacle. Given the Allies' overwhelming air superiority, Rommel knew that the Germans could no longer wage mobile warfare. "We must stop the enemy in the water," he told his commanders, "and destroy his equipment while it is still afloat."

Rommel brought to his new task the same unlimited energy and boundless ingenuity that he had brought to the desert war in North Africa. "The methods Rommel used to exploit the resources at his disposal were characteristic of his gift for improvisation," wrote Lieut. General Fritz Bayerlein, commander of the Panzer Lehr Division and former Afrikakorps chief of staff. "The new defense plan showed once again his complete independence of orthodox doctrine and systems."

Convinced that the first twenty-four hours of the invasion would be decisive, Rommel declared that the exposed beaches would be his *Hauptkampflinie*, or main line of battle. With this in mind, he set about deepening the German defenses. The Allied troops would have to brave thickets of underwater obstacles, many of them mined. Once ashore, they would be trapped within a five- to six-mile-deep "zone of death," massively mined and dotted with infantry and artillery strongpoints, backed up by panzer divisions, dug in to protect them from Allied bombers.

Rommel spent long hours touring the front. "He got up early, traveled fast, saw things very quickly, and seemed to have an instinct for the places where something was wrong," commented his naval adviser, Admiral Friedrich Ruge. In order to make certain the field commanders fully understood his plans, Rommel frequently drew sketches and diagrams. Several of the drawings can be seen on the following pages, published here for the first time.

Fortunately for the Allies, Rommel never had the free hand that he enjoyed in North Africa; in addition, he was short of troops, supplies, and time. Despite his enormous efforts, by June 1944, only a fraction of his proposed defenses were complete.

Field Marshal Erwin Rommel inspects the concrete antitank obstacles that he intended to use offshore against Allied landing craft. Rommel's ability to improvise impressed even his own engineering expert, General Wilhelm Meise, who called the field marshal the "greatest engineer of World War II."

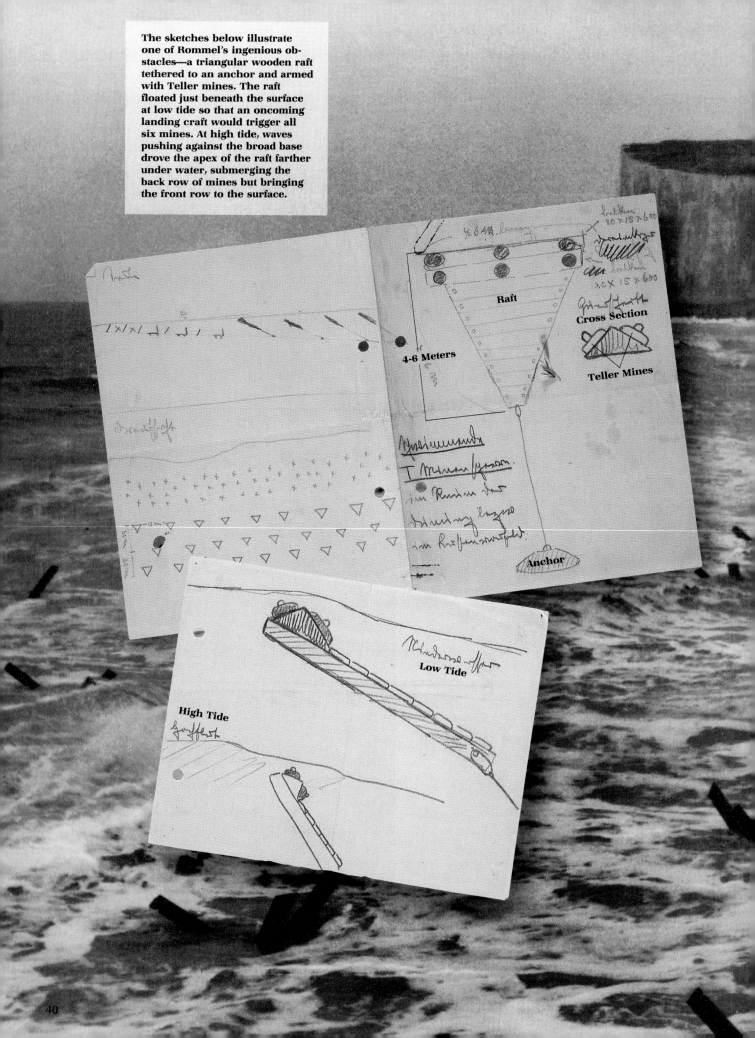

The sketches below illustrate one of Rommel's ingenious obstacles—a triangular wooden raft tethered to an anchor and armed with Teller mines. The raft floated just beneath the surface at low tide so that an oncoming landing craft would trigger all six mines. At high tide, waves pushing against the broad base drove the apex of the raft farther under water, submerging the back row of mines but bringing the front row to the surface.

Old antitank obstacles called hedgehogs bristle in the surf off a village in northern France. They were made of steel girders that had been bent at right angles and welded together.

Obstructions to Thwart Invaders

Rommel's most important innovation was his use of offshore obstacles placed between the high- and low-tide marks as artificial reefs to slow down or destroy incoming Allied landing craft.

These new underwater obstructions filled in the gaps between German strongpoints and shielded even the remotest stretches of the Channel coast. Often improvised out of captured enemy equipment, they came in a variety of shapes and sizes. The simplest were wooden stakes slanted seaward in shallow water, many of them tipped with antitank mines. There were also tetrahedrons, concrete dragon's teeth, V-shape ramps, curved metal rails, antitank barriers called Belgian gates, and other deadly devices.

Rommel installed 517,000 obstacles, equipping 31,000 with mines or shells. He had hoped to lay four belts so that two of them would always be beneath the surface. But only the two belts closest to shore were completed before D-day.

Strongpoints amid the Minefields

The cornerstone of Rommel's defensive system was his massive use of mines. The idea was rooted in his two years of experience fighting in North Africa, especially along the Gazala Line, at Tobruk and El Alamein. "We have learned in our engagements with the British," he wrote, "that large minefields with isolated strongpoints dispersed within them are extremely difficult to take." Thus, Rommel concentrated his troops behind such defenses. Backed up by dug-in tanks and artillery, these small fortresses presented formidable obstacles, even when manned by his ill-equipped, understrength coastal defense divi-

sions. "If the enemy should ever set foot on land," he wrote, "an attack through the minefields against the defense works sited within them will present him with a task of immense difficulty." Rommel needed an estimated 20 million mines to implement his plan of laying 10 mines per yard over two areas 1,000 yards deep, one along the coast, another along the land front five to six miles inland. He needed 180 million more to fill in between—an impossible goal given the limited time, the scarcity of mines, and the difficulties of transporting them to the beaches. In order to augment the supply, Rommel organized local mine-making factories and raided depots and arsenals for old French shells. During the four and half months before D-day, the Germans laid approximately 4.1 million mines on the Channel coast.

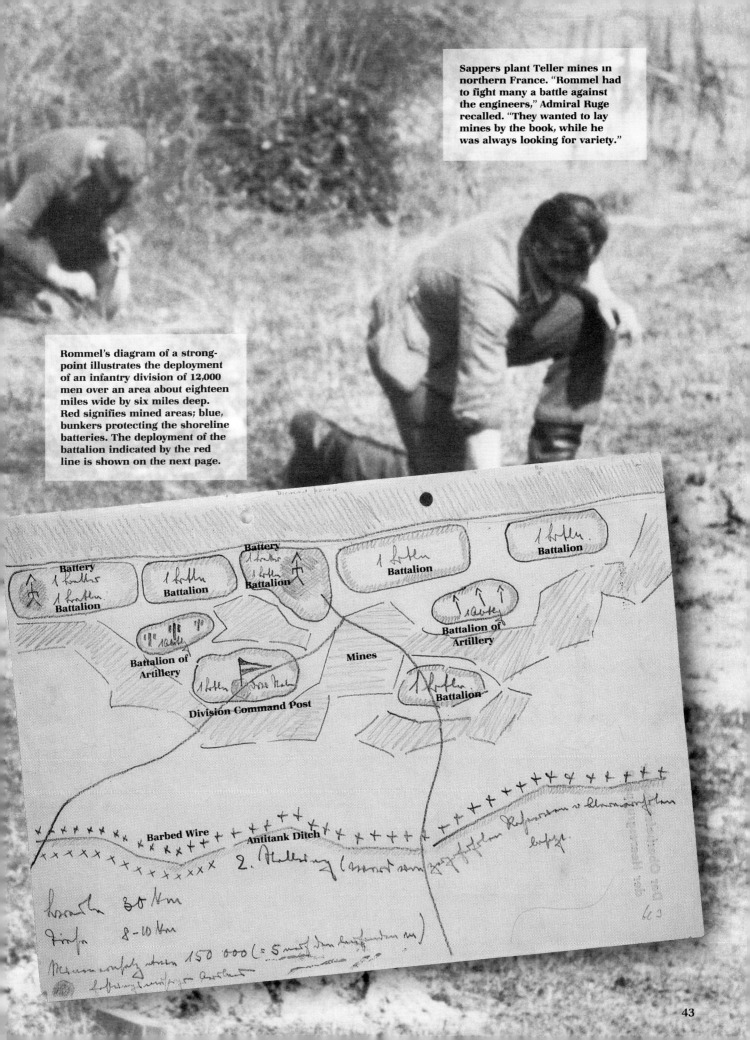

Sappers plant Teller mines in northern France. "Rommel had to fight many a battle against the engineers," Admiral Ruge recalled. "They wanted to lay mines by the book, while he was always looking for variety."

Rommel's diagram of a strongpoint illustrates the deployment of an infantry division of 12,000 men over an area about eighteen miles wide by six miles deep. Red signifies mined areas; blue, bunkers protecting the shoreline batteries. The deployment of the battalion indicated by the red line is shown on the next page.

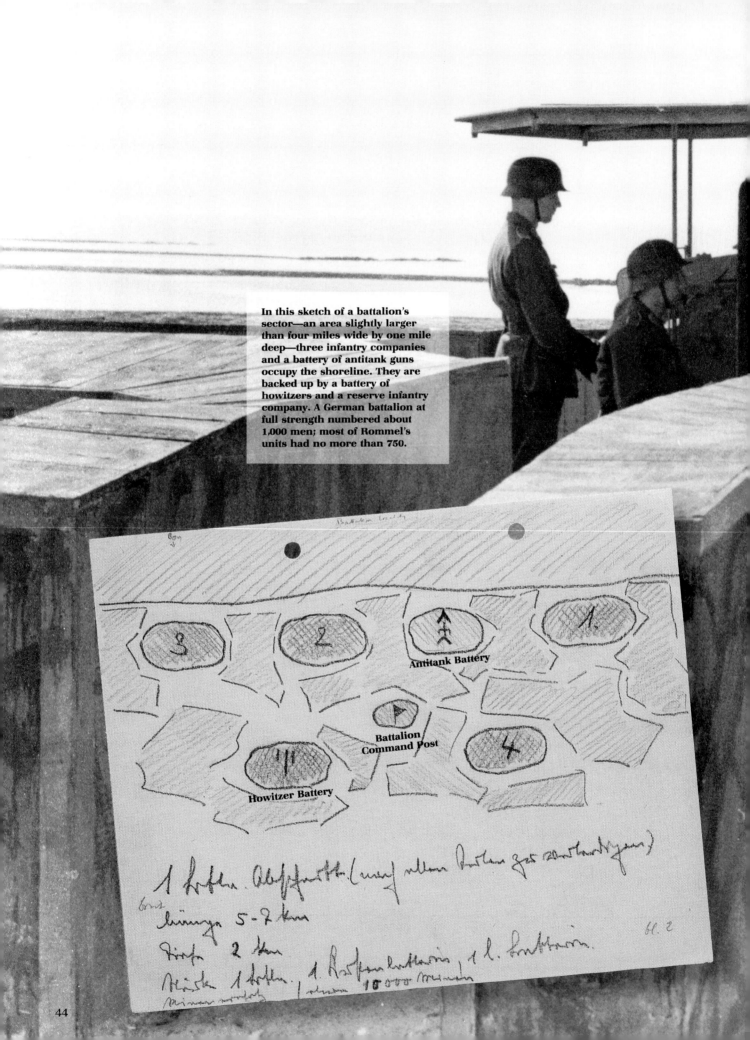

In this sketch of a battalion's sector—an area slightly larger than four miles wide by one mile deep—three infantry companies and a battery of antitank guns occupy the shoreline. They are backed up by a battery of howitzers and a reserve infantry company. A German battalion at full strength numbered about 1,000 men; most of Rommel's units had no more than 750.

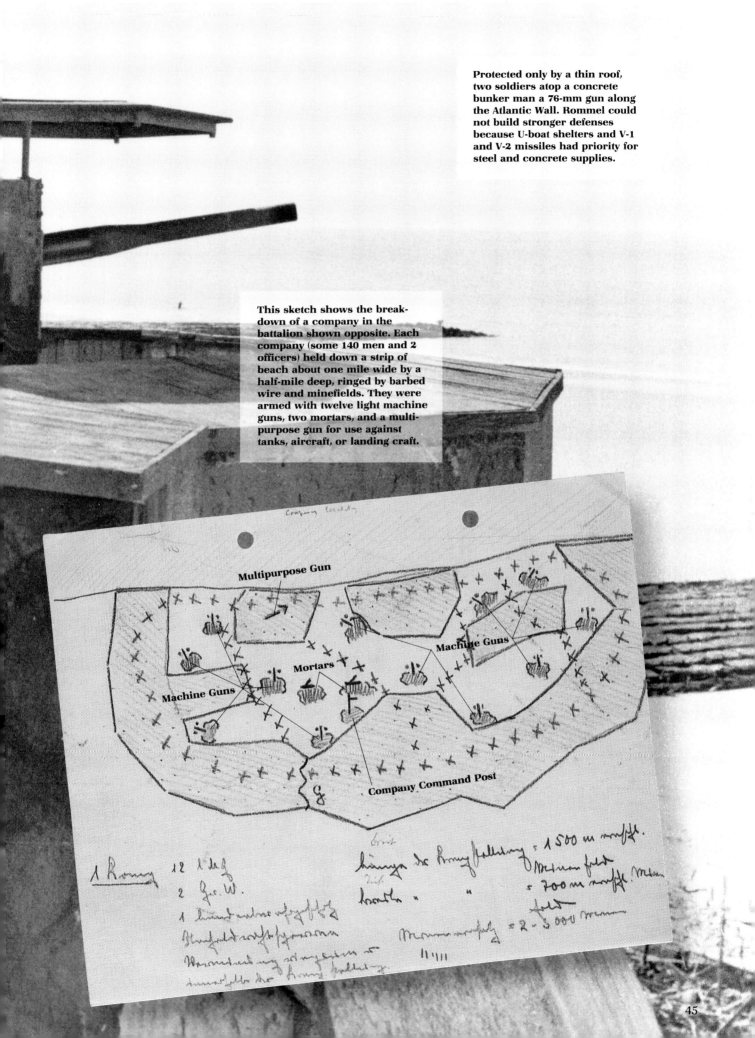

Protected only by a thin roof, two soldiers atop a concrete bunker man a 76-mm gun along the Atlantic Wall. Rommel could not build stronger defenses because U-boat shelters and V-1 and V-2 missiles had priority for steel and concrete supplies.

This sketch shows the breakdown of a company in the battalion shown opposite. Each company (some 140 men and 2 officers) held down a strip of beach about one mile wide by a half-mile deep, ringed by barbed wire and minefields. They were armed with twelve light machine guns, two mortars, and a multipurpose gun for use against tanks, aircraft, or landing craft.

Multipurpose Gun

Machine Guns

Mortars

Machine Guns

Company Command Post

TWO

The Struggle to Contain the Beachheads

The morning after D-day, the hopes of Field Marshal Erwin Rommel for driving the Allies back into the sea rode on his beloved panzers. The swift and powerful German armor with its superbly trained crews had earned him battle laurels on these very Normandy roads in 1940 and had helped him win lasting fame as the Desert Fox in North Africa. Now, on June 7, as he raced from unit to unit to rally his forces against the Allied invasion that had erupted in his absence the previous day—stopping only to dive for cover as British and American planes bombed and strafed—he counted on the panzers to crush the Allied beachheads.

Rommel was fairly certain of the Allies' immediate objectives as they attempted to break free of their D-day beachheads. His own battle-tested intuition, augmented by captured documents, correctly indicated that those objectives lay at the extreme flanks of the front. On his far left, the Americans would attempt to link up their two separate beachheads around the city of Carentan, pivot northward into the Cotentin Peninsula, and push to the port of Cherbourg, as Rommel himself had done in 1940. On his far right, the British and Canadians would hammer southward at the old university city of Caen, a road and rail hub that pointed the way toward Paris, some 120 miles to the southeast.

The terrain dictated differing strategies for Rommel's defensive plan. To the west, Rommel would depend on what the French called the *bocage*—a patchwork of small fields enclosed by thick, raised hedgerows—to slow the American advance. To the east, however, the bocage thinned, and to the south and east of Caen, the landscape gradually opened up, giving way to gently rolling hills that were ideal for British armor intent on breaking out into the heart of France and cutting off the German line of retreat.

The Germans squandered an opportunity to strike an early blow to the invaders. On the morning of June 6, Field Marshal Gerd von Rundstedt, the Paris-based commander in chief West, issued orders for the strategic reserve—12th SS Panzer Division and Panzer Lehr Division—to move forward and join the 21st Panzer Division near Caen for a counterattack directed at the gap between the British and Canadians north of the city. Those

Laden with ammunition, a machine-gun crew of the 12th SS Panzer (Hitlerjugend) Division prepares for battle. Indoctrinated to consider the war a "struggle for the survival of the German race," these teenagers had their baptism of fire in Normandy.

47

orders were countermanded, however, by General Alfred Jodl, OKW chief of staff, who feared that the Normandy landings were merely a feint and that the main invasion would come elsewhere.

Rommel, Rundstedt's subordinate, also made the same desperate request, to no avail. Not until midafternoon did Hitler finally agree to release the reserves, and by then, the Allies had consolidated their beachheads. Rommel's armor had lost invaluable time. All he could do when he arrived from Germany on the evening of the 6th was act quickly to get the delayed counterattack under way and salvage the situation.

The strongest of the armored formations was the Panzer Lehr Division. Organized from *Lehr*, or demonstration, units at the panzer training schools, the division had been formed expressly to repel an invasion of France. Probably the only panzer division in the German army operating at full strength, it fielded 149 tanks and assault guns and more than 612 armored personnel carriers, self-propelled guns, and other tracked vehicles. Its commander, Lieut. General Fritz Bayerlein, was Rommel's old chief of staff in the Afrikakorps, and many of its men had served in North Africa and in Russia. Bayerlein proudly recalled the words of Germany's leading panzer strategist, General Heinz Guderian, who had told him in April, "With this division alone, you will throw the Anglo-Americans back into the sea."

But first, Panzer Lehr had to reach the battlefield. Guderian, accustomed to freewheeling on the steppes of Russia without concern for air attacks, had not reckoned with such overwhelming Allied supremacy in the skies. At 5:00 p.m. on D-day, Panzer Lehr moved out from its position in reserve near Le Mans, headed for the front 130 miles away. It was not long before its five separate columns were running a fiery gantlet of air attacks. The long summer day lit the landscape until nearly midnight, and American and British fighter-bombers turned Lehr's path into what one German officer described as a "witch's cauldron." The aircraft smashed bridges, cratered crossroads, set villages ablaze, picked off grenadiers riding in the open half-tracks, and bombed the panzers, which tried to hide behind camouflage and the fringes of forests.

Such attacks cost the division 130 trucks, 5 tanks, and 84 other tracked vehicles before it ever went into battle. And the aerial raiders almost cost Lehr its commander. Bayerlein threw himself into a ditch just before 20-mm shells from strafing aircraft killed his driver and turned his BMW staff car into a twisted and charred steel skeleton. Looking skyward and seeing only Allied aircraft and almost never the Luftwaffe, the panzer crews began to joke grimly that American and British planes were painted silver, but German ones had a special coating that made them invisible.

It was not until the afternoon of June 7 that the lead elements of Panzer

A German soldier hurls a gre-
nade during close-range fighting
for Bayeux, a small city five
miles south of the Channel coast.
On June 7, 1944, Bayeux became
the first sizable French town
to be liberated by the Allies.

Lehr limped up to the front, where they found that Rommel's planned counterattack had failed to materialize. Of the other two divisions involved, the 21st Panzer had only seventy tanks available after its exertions on D-day. The 12th SS Panzer Division had been sorely delayed, like Panzer Lehr, by air attacks during its sixty-five-mile trip from Lisieux, and only a single battle group had reached the front.

That vanguard, however, was in position just west of Caen and ready to deliver a surprise blow. The 12th was known as the Hitlerjugend, or Hitler Youth, Division because most of its members had been recruited from that organization. Their average age was a bit over eighteen, and although the young volunteers were untested in combat, they were fanatical in their devotion to the Führer.

Their battle group that day consisted of a battalion of Panzer IV medium tanks and three infantry battalions under the command of SS Colonel Kurt

Meyer. Nicknamed "Panzer" for his drive and swashbuckling style, Meyer was a fervent Nazi and a resourceful veteran of three years on the Russian front, where he cultivated the habit of leading his men into combat on a motorcycle. On this afternoon, he was foiling the enemy planes that attacked his fuel trucks by organizing a fleet of *Kübelwagens*, small and maneuverable cars, to carry forward the precious fluid in jerry cans.

Meyer also boasted that his young fanatics would force the British back, and he looked for a good observation post from which to locate his enemy. He found a superb spot in one of the turrets of the Abbey of Ardenne, situated on the western outskirts of Caen. From there, he could see Sherman tanks of the Canadian 3d Infantry Division moving up near the Carpiquet airfield, a couple of miles west of Caen. Over his field telephone, Meyer arranged an ambush. His rookie force waited patiently behind a hedge on the exposed flank of the Canadian armor until the lead tanks came within 200 yards. Then, at Meyer's command, his antitank gunners opened up, his panzers advanced, and his grenadiers pounced on the enemy infantry. The German shells struck the thirty-six-ton Shermans on their thinner side armor with deadly effect. Within minutes, the young gunners shot up twenty-eight Shermans. Meyer's men drove the surprised Canadians back two miles before Allied field artillery and naval gunfire succeeded in forcing them to break off the attack.

This fierce little action was a forecast of the zest for combat the Hitler Youth would demonstrate in the coming weeks. In Normandy and beyond, they would fight with such dedication that the division eventually would suffer 90 percent casualties, while gaining notoriety for gunning down prisoners of war—a breach of the rules of warfare not limited to the Germans. Meyer himself would soon take command of the entire 12th SS Panzer, becoming, at age thirty-three, the youngest division commander in

An armored column from the 12th SS Panzer Division rolls through a French town on June 8, 1944, heading for a confrontation with the Canadian 3d Infantry Division located west of Caen. Their orders were to attack the enemy and "throw him back into the sea."

the Germany army. But that night after their first action, many of the young soldiers wept tears of frustration because they had not in fact driven the enemy all the way back into the sea.

During the following days, the Allies gradually consolidated and expanded their beachheads. In the German center, the Americans broke through the lines of the 352d Infantry Division, which earlier had defended Omaha Beach with so much determination. The forces of the U.S. V Corps captured the town of Isigny and drove on toward the key city of Carentan. Other V Corps units linked up in the center with the British at Port-en-Bessin and penetrated southward toward Caumont. The British, facing tougher opposition on the German right, took Bayeux, five miles inland, and drove on southeastward into the area west of Caen.

On June 8, Rommel tried once again to mass his panzers for a decisive

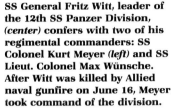

SS General Fritz Witt, leader of the 12th SS Panzer Division, (center) confers with two of his regimental commanders: SS Colonel Kurt Meyer (left) and SS Lieut. Colonel Max Wünsche. After Witt was killed by Allied naval gunfire on June 16, Meyer took command of the division.

blow on his right against the British and a breakthrough to the sea. His three armored divisions were to strike northward between Bayeux and Caen. But this time the counterattack had to be postponed because the new headquarters for Panzer Group West under General Leo Geyr von Schweppenburg had not yet been established. And when they got under way, the panzers collided head-on with a major British armored attack and came under devastating fire from offshore ships.

On June 10, Allied air supremacy completely disrupted further plans for an armored counteroffensive. Rommel, en route to Geyr's headquarters to confer about the planned attack, had to abandon his car and take cover no fewer than thirty times. Then, a few hours after Rommel's departure, British Typhoon fighter-bombers and medium Mitchell bombers attacked the command center. The Allies had been alerted to its location on a farm a dozen miles south of Caen through radio intercepts and aerial reconnaissance. And the Allied airmen had no trouble distinguishing the headquarters, since General Geyr—a veteran of the Russian front who had yet to learn about Allied air power—had neglected to order it camouflaged. Geyr escaped with minor wounds, but his headquarters was demolished, and practically his entire operations staff was killed or wounded.

Rommel now shifted to the defensive, concentrating on the east. By the end of the first week, he had deployed some 520 panzers against the British

A company from the Panther battalion of the Panzer Lehr Division awaits orders in a field near Tilly on June 10. The 50-ton Panthers were so powerful that the Allies needed four or five Cromwell or Sherman tanks to destroy one of them.

His head bandaged from a shell-fragment wound, SS Lieut. Colonel Max Wünsche, commander of the 12th SS Panzer Regiment, rides a motorcycle to the main German aid station. Beside him in the sidecar is Lieutenant Rudolf von Ribbentrop, son of the Nazi foreign minister, whose arm had been hit during a strafing attack.

between Caumont and Caen, as compared with only about 70 in the west. But having failed to crush the enemy on the beaches and finding himself woefully short of infantry, he had to commit his panzers piecemeal to plug gaps and prevent a breakout in the line that now stretched for more than fifty miles. The armored personnel carriers of Panzer Lehr were parked behind the front; the division's panzergrenadiers and tank crews, instead of massing for decisive thrusts against the enemy, took up static positions on a ten-mile-wide front in the bocage country west of Caen.

This was a new kind of warfare for the proud panzer crews. Their machines served basically as strongpoints established in the hedgerows and sunken farm lanes worn down by cattle and wagons. The hedgerows, originally planted to mark property boundaries and shield crops from ocean winds, were dense with trees and bushes firmly rooted in earthen dikes three or four feet thick and about as high. Allied tanks attempting to plow through these hedgerows reared up and exposed their vulnerable underbellies. They then became easy targets for the guns of the panzers

concealed nearby or for the powerful arsenal of the grenadiers dug in alongside them—weapons that ranged from the hand-held *Panzerfaust* to the dual-purpose 88-mm flak and antitank gun.

Within the confines of this new kind of armored warfare, small but spectacular battles erupted, prompting Rommel to describe the campaign as "one terrible bloodletting." Perhaps the most remarkable such action occurred on June 13, a week after the invasion and three days after Rommel abandoned the idea of an armored counterattack. A gap had opened in the German line opposite the juncture of the British and American sectors. To the left of the gap, Rommel's troops were preoccupied with stopping the U.S. V Corps, which had penetrated seventeen miles inland and captured Caumont, located on high ground some twenty miles southwest of Caen. To the right of the gap, the western flank of Panzer Lehr was anchored near the village of Tilly-sur-Seulles.

Into this breach knifed a spearhead of the British 7th Armored Division, the famed Desert Rats who had bedeviled Rommel in North Africa. The British column of tanks and motorized infantry swept around the left flank of their old North African foe, Fritz Bayerlein, and into Villers-Bocage, a crossroads village six miles east of Caumont and about fifteen miles southwest of Caen. These Desert Rats were now a half-dozen or so miles behind Panzer Lehr's left flank at Tilly and ready to drive northeastward toward Caen and encircle the German armor.

About midmorning, however, the British were spotted by SS Lieutenant Michael Wittmann, commander of a company of Tiger tanks. Wittmann's outfit, the 101st SS Heavy Tank Battalion, had recently arrived from near Paris after a harrowing journey under air attack. Wittmann was the German army's leading tank ace. On the Russian front, he had destroyed no fewer than 117 tanks and won the coveted Knight's Cross with Oak Leaves. He was reconnoitering the high ground just northeast of Villers-Bocage that morning when he saw the procession of British Cromwell tanks and half-tracked vehicles leave the village.

Wittmann's sixty-three-ton Tiger had armor four inches thick on its turret and packed a gun so powerful that its shells could penetrate steel plate at a range of 1,000 yards. Confident that the Cromwell's 75-mm shells would bounce off harmlessly, Wittmann bore down at point-blank range.

His first shots stopped the British column cold, and he spent the remainder of the day disabling Cromwell after Cromwell. Joined in the afternoon by a number of other panzers, Wittmann raised havoc in Villers-Bocage. By the end of the day, infantry from Panzer Lehr and from the 2d SS Panzer Division, which was coming forward to plug the gap west of Lehr, secured the victory, driving the Desert Rats from the village. Almost single-

Lieutenant Wittmann's One-Man War

SS Lieutenant Michael Wittmann displays the Knight's Cross with Oak Leaves that he won after destroying 117 Soviet tanks. Later, in Normandy, Wittmann would be decorated anew for his exploits against the British.

On the morning of June 13, 1944, SS Lieutenant Michael Wittmann, a thirty-year-old company commander in the 101st SS Heavy Tank Battalion, stood in the turret of his Tiger tank and peered through field glasses at the landscape southwest of Caen. Approaching along the highway from the nearby town of Villers-Bocage was a British armored column. While its leading tank squadron rolled forward to scout the terrain, the motorized infantry company directly behind the tanks halted alongside the road.

"They're acting as if they have won the war already," growled Wittmann's gunner, angered by the enemy's seeming nonchalance. "We're going to prove them wrong," Wittmann declared.

Wittmann moved quickly. He radioed the rest of his company to attack the tank squadron, then ordered his driver to maneuver his Tiger into firing position in a grove overlooking the highway. Sensing the opportunity for an unprecedented kill, Wittmann let loose with his 88-mm gun, turning the lead British half-track into a burning hulk that blocked the highway.

Wittmann's Tiger then rumbled the length of the trapped column, firing at will from point-blank range. In less than ten minutes, he had destroyed dozens of vehicles.

But the Germans were far from finished. As other panzers arrived to take prisoners, Wittmann organized a number of them and pressed ahead to Villers-Bocage. The British infantry was waiting for them. In the fierce struggle that ensued, an antitank projectile knocked the track off Wittmann's Tiger. Undeterred, he kept on firing until he had destroyed every enemy target within range. Then, he escaped on foot—only to return later with fifteen more panzers to continue the fight. At the end of the day, Wittmann was credited with destroying twenty-five British tanks and twenty-eight other vehicles.

His heroics earned him the rare swords honor to his Knight's Cross and a promotion to captain. But Wittmann had little time to enjoy his laurels. Eight weeks later, he suffered the same fate as his numerous victims: He was killed in a tank battle south of Caen.

Smashed half-tracks of the
British 4th County of London
Yeomanry lie demolished near
the entrance to Villers-Bocage.

British soldiers killed by
Wittmann's tanks line a ditch
along the road to Villers-Bocage.

After the battle, Wittmann's disabled and burned-out Tiger tank sits amid the rubble in Villers-Bocage. Whenever possible, the British torched the interiors of abandoned panzers so that the Germans could not salvage them.

handedly, Wittmann and his crew had thwarted the British attempt to entrap Panzer Lehr and dashed the Allied hopes of cracking open the developing stalemate around Caen.

On the far left of the front, meanwhile, Rommel was even less prepared to frustrate the Allies' intentions. The Americans' first major objective there was the town of Carentan, which lay athwart the road to the strategic port of Cherbourg and was the prospective location for the linkup of troops from Utah and Omaha beaches. For four days, the battle between elite airborne forces raged in the hedgerows and swamps around Carentan. Elements of the U.S. 101st Airborne Division attacked from north and east against the crack 6th Paratroop Regiment under Lieut. Colonel Friedrich-August von der Heydte, a hero of the German airborne invasion of Crete in 1941.

Although the hedgerows afforded excellent cover, converting each farm field into a separate little battleground, Heydte's paratroopers soon found themselves in an untenable situation. They were outnumbered—one of his battalions had 25 men left out of 700—and short of ammunition, despite a rare supply drop by a flight of Ju 52 transport planes. Promised reinforcements had been delayed by Allied air interdiction. During the night of June 11, Heydte felt such pressure from enemy troops already in the town as well as from artillery and naval gunfire that he disobeyed orders and abandoned Carentan—a prudent action, though one that probably would have resulted in a court martial but for his previous record.

His retreat allowed the U.S. V and VII corps to join forces and forge a solid bridgehead some sixty miles wide and ten miles deep. And indirectly, the

Wearing their distinctive bowl-shape helmets, members of the German 6th Paratroop Regiment tend a wounded comrade in a barn near Carentan. The other soldiers are SS panzergrenadiers who fought side by side with the paratroopers.

withdrawal cost the Germans one of their most brilliant commanders. On June 12, General Erich Marcks, commander of the LXXXIV Corps and an architect of the invasion of Russia, where he had lost a leg in combat, set out to investigate reports that Carentan had fallen. An enemy aircraft swooped down on his car with guns blazing. Marcks, hobbled by a wooden leg, failed to scramble for cover in time and was killed. That day and the next, the 17th SS Panzergrenadier Division counterattacked to recapture Carentan, but its effort came too late, and the Americans kept the town.

The American occupation of Carentan set the stage for a full-scale drive toward Cherbourg and created a dilemma for Rommel. Should he weaken his lines in front of Caen by removing troops to reinforce this newly endangered front in the west? Before the invasion, Hitler had expressed his belief that the loss of a major port constituted the most dangerous threat to the security of Fortress Europe. But Rommel opted for blocking the British at Caen. The forces on the Cotentin Peninsula, he decided, would have to make do with fragments of three divisions augmented only by the recently arrived 77th Infantry Division.

The Americans launched their offensive toward Cherbourg on June 14 from Sainte-Mère-Église, eight miles north of Carentan. Attacking with two divisions, they hoped to drive westward and lop off the Cotentin Peninsula at its twenty-five-mile-wide base. Under the lash of the U.S. VII Corps commander, Lieut. General J. Lawton Collins, who had won the nickname "Lightning Joe" for his drive and quickness in the Pacific, they penetrated more than halfway across the peninsula in three days, astonishing German generals whose previous combat experience against the Americans had suggested they moved only after great deliberation.

On June 17, Hitler came to France to meet with his top two commanders for the first time since the invasion began. Rommel and his superior, Gerd von Rundstedt, had asked for the conference in an attempt to open Hitler's eyes to the problems of containing the Allied armies. Ironically, the meeting took place near Soissons, 150 miles east of the Normandy battleground, in the elaborate complex of bombproof bunkers built at the height of German success in 1940 to serve as Hitler's field headquarters for the invasion of England that never materialized. The Führer, fiddling nervously with pencils used to color maps and sitting on a stool while his field marshals stood, refused their requests for freedom of action. There would be no withdrawals, even for tactical reasons. He reiterated his earlier dogma about fixed defense—"Every man shall fight or fall where he stands"—and ordered that "fortress Cherbourg be held at any cost."

Hitler tried to encourage his commanders with talk of new superweapons, including the V-1 flying bombs first launched against London five days previously. The man in charge of the so-called Vengeance Weapons, General Erich Heinemann, was present, and Rommel and Rundstedt suggested to him that the flying bombs be flung against the Allied beachheads in Normandy. Impossible, replied Heinemann. The guidance system was not accurate enough to employ the V-1 against tactical targets; the typical margin of error—up to a dozen miles—would endanger friendly forces.

Confirmation of that likelihood came presently. Rommel and Rundstedt tried to persuade Hitler to visit a headquarters near the front on the following day. They noted that the British prime minister, Winston Churchill, had visited his beachheads a few days earlier. A personal appearance by Hitler, who liked to boast of his front-line duty during the First World War, would not only hearten German troops but also give the Führer firsthand experience of the adverse conditions under which they were fighting. Hitler agreed to go, but soon after the two commanders left his bunker, one of the V-1s went awry in its flight toward London, took a U-turn, and landed directly above the bunker. Safely ensconced under twenty-two feet of concrete, Hitler escaped injury. But he hurried back to Germany the next morning without paying a visit to the front-line troops.

In any event, Hitler would not have been able to visit the defenders on the Cotentin Peninsula. Early on the morning of June 18, they were cut off when the U.S. VII Corps reached the Atlantic coast near the resort town of Barneville, completing a corridor all the way across the base of the peninsula. The peninsula's defenders were now separated from the main body of the LXXXIV Corps, and trapped.

One of the units isolated on the peninsula, the newly arrived 77th Infantry Division, was a first-class fighting formation. Rommel had anticipated the direction of the American thrust four days previously and attempted to save the 77th from the entrapment. But his orders to the division to break out to the south ran counter to the fortress mentality of Hitler, who first countermanded Rommel's directive and insisted the division stand fast, and then modified his own orders.

The resulting confusion doomed much, but not all, of the 77th Division. Acting on belated orders from army headquarters, Major General Rudolf Stegmann tried to move parts of the division southward through the American corridor on the morning of June 18. But the attempt was thwarted, and Stegmann was killed instantly in an attack by Allied fighter-bombers—the fourth German general to die in action since the invasion.

Colonel Rudolf Bacherer took command and, during the following night, led 1,500 men on a stealthy march through American lines just east of Barneville. On the afternoon of June 19, just when he thought his column was safe, Bacherer encountered an enemy-held bridge at the Ollande River,

Accompanied by aides, Adolf Hitler and Field Marshal Erwin Rommel walk to a rendezvous with Field Marshal Gerd von Rundstedt in northeast France on June 17, 1944. Rommel and Rundstedt had requested the conference to inform the Führer of the plight of their armies.

five miles southeast of Barneville. He ordered his men to fix bayonets, and supported by a light machine gun, they charged the bridge and carried it. With more than 100 prisoners and twelve captured jeeps, these survivors of the 77th crossed proudly into friendly lines.

North of the American corridor, meanwhile, their isolated comrades undertook the dubious task of delaying the American drive against Cher-

bourg. The German commander on the peninsula, Lieut. General Karl-Wilhelm von Schlieben, had the remnants of his own 709th Division and fragments of two others, along with a few old French tanks captured during the campaign of 1940. He faced three divisions of the reorganized U.S. VII Corps that were pushing northward up the peninsula. Meanwhile, the newly activated U.S. VIII Corps sealed off the rear against any German thrusts from the south. After mounting a resistance for a few days, most of Schlieben's makeshift forces retreated on the night of June 19 within the semicircle of fortifications several miles in front of Cherbourg.

The defenses of Cherbourg, though designed primarily to meet a threat from the sea, nonetheless appeared to be formidable obstacles to the Americans pressing in on the city's three landward sides. Antitank ditches and concrete pillboxes and other strongpoints studded the three ridges guarding the approaches to the city. But in fact, the defenses were not strongly manned. The curving German perimeter stretched for a distance of some thirty miles, and the 25,000 defenders now at General Schlieben's disposal included such noncombatants as naval clerks, Luftwaffe ground staff, and civilian construction workers. And even among his combat troops, one man in five was a foreigner; the non-Germans included Poles and Russians conscripted during the German conquest of their countries. Hitler's orders were to defend the "honor of the German army." But as Schlieben noted later, "You can't expect Russians and Poles to fight for Germany against Americans in France."

The Americans probed Cherbourg's perimeter for two days and then launched an all-out attack on June 22. A powerful storm that had ravaged the English Channel during the past three days gave special urgency to the swift capture of Cherbourg port facilities; wind and waves had wrecked hundreds of landing craft and severely damaged the two artificial harbors called Mulberries that were considered vital to supplying the Allied beach-heads. As if to punctuate this new immediacy, an Allied air assault of more than 1,000 planes preceded the ground attack. The "air pulverization," as General Collins called it, stunned and demoralized the defenders in their fortifications, but the Germans managed to shoot down 29 aircraft and to hold off significant infantry penetration for at least a day. The Americans could move forward only a pillbox at a time, firing bazooka shells into the apertures and getting in close enough to lay demolition charges.

Schlieben knew his makeshift garrison could not long maintain resistance, but he desperately wanted to buy time for German naval engineers to destroy the harbor and thus deny it to the Americans. He tried to bolster spirits by freely handing out Iron Cross medals specially airdropped by the Luftwaffe. But by June 25, his defenses were collapsing all around him, and

the enemy had a foothold in the city. Allied ships then joined in the assault, hurling shells from three battleships, four cruisers, and eleven destroyers until counterfire from German shore batteries drove them back.

That afternoon, Schlieben radioed a plaintive plea to Rommel: "Enemy superiority in matériel and enemy domination of the air overwhelming. Troops badly exhausted. Harbor effectively destroyed. Have 2,000 wounded without possibility of moving them. Is there any point in having our remaining forces entirely wiped out?"

Rommel replied: "In accordance with the Führer's orders, you are to continue fighting to the last cartridge."

On June 26, with enemy tank destroyers firing directly into the entrances of his underground command post, Schlieben surrendered himself and 800 other occupants. Pockets of resistance held out for four additional days before the Americans could claim possession of the entire peninsula.

Cherbourg was theirs—but more than a week behind schedule, the harbor in ruins. Dock machinery had been destroyed, the harbor mined, and the port basins so crammed with sunken ships and 20,000 cubic yards of masonry rubble that Cherbourg would require more than three months to become fully operational again. "A masterful job," an American engineer concerned with the port's rehabilitation wrote ruefully, "beyond a doubt, the most complete, intensive, and best-planned demolition in history."

Hitler was so enraged at what he regarded as the premature collapse of resistance at Cherbourg that he looked for a scapegoat. He ordered the court martial of General Friedrich Dollmann, Rommel's sixty-two-year-old subordinate, who had commanded the Seventh Army for more than four years. Rundstedt intervened, calling instead for a court of inquiry. But the threat was too much for Dollmann, who was found dead on the morning of June 29. He was first reported as killed in action, then as the victim of a heart attack. Dollmann had been overweight and suffering from heart problems. Decades later, his chief of staff revealed that Dollmann had committed suicide by swallowing poison.

To emphasize the need to stand fast on the rest of the front, Hitler had summoned his western commanders to a meeting on June 29 at his mountain villa at Berchtesgaden. Forbidden by Hitler to fly because the Allies controlled the skies, Rommel and Rundstedt had to drive all night to get there and then were kept waiting for six hours. And Hitler, in fact, had nothing new to tell them. He was bitterly disappointed by the loss of Cherbourg. Troops were to stand fast no matter what. Jet aircraft and other superweapons would soon turn the tide. He still expected a second invasion along the Pas-de-Calais and insisted on keeping the 200,000 men of the Fifteenth Army there, even though reinforcements were desperately

needed 200 miles away in Normandy, where the Allies had landed more than 900,000 men and outnumbered the defenders by about three to one.

Rommel and Rundstedt repeatedly tried to raise larger questions with the Führer. The Reich should make peace in the west, they suggested, in order to concentrate on the onrushing Red Army in the east. Hitler told them to stick to fighting and leave political matters to him. When Rommel persisted in talking politics, Hitler asked him to leave the room. Rommel obeyed, and the two never met again.

The fighting around Caen, meanwhile, was reaching a peak. The battles in the eastern sector had mounted in intensity during the previous week as the British 11th Armored Division renewed Field Marshal Sir Bernard Law Montgomery's attempt to flank the city. On June 22, this newly landed division with its Sherman tanks had struck southward over the Odon River toward Hill 112, important high ground located a half-dozen miles southwest of Caen. The British tankers encountered the young fanatics of the 12th SS Panzer Division in fighting so fierce that even the newly promoted German division commander, Major General Kurt Meyer, got into the fray, shouldering a Panzerfaust antitank weapon.

Young German grenadiers lay in sunken lanes and behind hedgerows with their weapons at the ready. In one of the skirmishes, twenty-year-old Emil Dürr jumped up and fired his Panzerfaust into a Sherman tank, setting it ablaze. Then he flung a so-called sticky bomb against the side of another Sherman. This explosive, covered with adhesive coating, was supposed to stick to the tank, but it fell away. Dürr grabbed the bomb off the ground and held it against the side of the tank until it exploded, killing him and destroying the tank. Despite such individual heroism, the day was saved for the Germans by their tanks, which counterattacked and blunted the British drive.

Both sides were bringing up reinforcements and mapping major offensives. As early as June 20, Hitler had ordered a massive counterattack intended to smash the British bridgehead. The strike was to involve six armored divisions, including the panzer elite of the army. In preparation, four additional units were ordered to Normandy: the veteran 9th and 10th Panzer divisions of the II SS Panzer Corps from the eastern front, and the 276th and 277th Infantry divisions from southern France. The depleted Panzer Lehr and the 12th SS Panzer were to be relieved. But all of these reinforcements were repeatedly delayed by a transportation network so crippled by air attacks and sabotage by the French Resistance that it took one infantry battle group five days to travel 180 miles.

The British offensive, code-named Epsom and slated for June 22, was also delayed. The Channel storm had temporarily stopped the flow of men and supplies and forced Montgomery to postpone Epsom for several days. But he was propelled by a special urgency: Decoded German radio messages, provided by the British code-breaking system Ultra, revealed the movements of Rommel's rein-

Lieut. General Karl-Wilhelm von Schlieben, Cotentin Peninsula commander, and Rear Admiral Walther Hennecke, naval commander in Normandy, surrender on June 26. Though denounced by Hitler as incompetent, Schlieben had delayed the Americans long enough for Hennecke to demolish the port facilities.

forcements, and Montgomery was determined to strike before the German panzers could. On June 25, elements of one corps moved against Panzer Lehr just east of Tilly. The following day, farther east, Epsom's main force— an entire corps of nearly 60,000 men and 600 tanks—attacked southward on a four-mile-wide front just west of Caen. The goal, as in the smaller, unsuccessful thrust four days earlier, was to get across the Odon River, seize the high ground at Hill 112 southwest of Caen, and cut off that city.

SS panzergrenadiers observe Allied troop movements from behind a wall of ornamental stonework. The armored divisions carried the major burden of the German defense.

Blocking the British path, once more, were the teenagers of the 12th SS Panzer Division. They faced the Scottish 15th Division, one of the best in the British army, and the supporting 11th Armored Division. Meyer's youngsters were now so reduced in number that, at one point, the advancing British mistook their main body for a mere screen of snipers and machine guns. But they fought stubbornly from a three-tier network of defensive positions—a honeycomb of machine guns, mortars, and mine-fields—some five miles deep in the maze of hedgerows, sunken lanes, and cornfields north of the Odon. Through conventional tactics and desperate ones—some of the Germans tied explosives around their waists and jumped on British tanks—they managed to contain the British north of the Odon for two days. Then, the British seized a bridge and broke across the river with their tanks on the morning of June 28, heading for Hill 112.

German crew members operating *Panzerwerfer 42* self-propelled rocket launchers check their camouflaged equipment in a grove near Caen. Used primarily as a close-support weapon to lay down massed fire, the rocket launchers lacked the accuracy of field artillery but were more mobile.

In the midst of the crisis on June 28, the anxiously awaited panzer reinforcements arrived at last. General Paul Hausser, a veteran army commander and the ablest of the SS generals, finally completed the journey from Poland with the two divisions of his II SS Panzer Corps and prepared to counterattack almost immediately, on the morning of June 29.

His plan was to assault the right flank of the three-mile-wide Allied salient that now extended dangerously astride the Odon River. Hausser's two panzer divisions and part of another would drive on a northeast axis toward Caen. But the British again had been forewarned of German intentions by Ultra decodes and by a document in the possession of a captured SS officer. When Hausser's 250 panzers began assembling for the attack at 7:00 a.m., they came under furious air assault as well as what he described as "murderous fire from naval guns in the Channel and the terrible British artillery." The 16-inch naval shells exploded with such impact that they upended even the sixty-three-ton Tiger tanks; artillery fire

was so intense that some of the panzer crewmen believed the British were using some new kind of self-loading guns. Doomed before it began, the attack finally got under way hours late that afternoon and then sputtered under the brunt of British antitank guns and still more shelling.

The British, unaware that Hausser's momentum was all but exhausted, grew cautious and began withdrawing from their bridgehead across the Odon on June 30. The little river was virtually dammed with the dead of both sides—Meyer alone lost 800 men and the Scottish 15th Division more than 2,300. A couple of miles to the southeast, the blackened slopes of Hill 112 presented similar scenes of death and desolation. British tanks had clambered to the top of this vital eminence during Hausser's failed counterattack the previous day, and at dawn, Hausser's panzers returned the

Blasted tree stumps and wrecked Sherman tanks from the British 4th Armored Brigade testify to the ferocity of the fighting for Hill 112, a vital observation post southwest of Caen. The Germans nicknamed the tortured ground the "grove of half-trees."

favor, dislodging the Shermans with the help of the 7th Mortar Brigade and its *Nebelwerfers*, the ingenious, multibarreled weapons that flung thousands of screaming rocket-propelled charges onto the devastated hilltop.

On that same day, June 30, Rommel returned to the front from his meeting with Hitler to find what his staff reported as "complete defensive success." Hausser's panzers had stopped the British attempt at a breakthrough, but they had failed to achieve the decisive blow Hitler had originally contemplated to crush the Allies. That afternoon, after the German armor had been rebuffed once again, Rommel's panzer chief, General Geyr, and Hausser, now acting commander of Seventh Army, both prepared remarkably similar and pessimistic assessments. In order to move out of range of the lethal enemy naval guns, shorten their line, and make possible the creation of a mobile panzer reserve, they wrote, the German defenders should execute a limited tactical withdrawal from the Caen salient. Rommel and Rundstedt each endorsed these recommendations and passed them on to Hitler, who, on July 1, predictably fired back the familiar injunction: "Present positions are to be held."

But Rundstedt pushed further. On the telephone that evening with Field Marshal Wilhelm Keitel, chief of the armed forces high command, he sketched such a gloomy picture of conditions in Normandy that Keitel cried out in despair, "What shall we do?" Rundstedt, according to his chief of staff, had a ready reply: "Make peace, you fools! What else can you do?"

The next morning, at about the time that Geyr was relieved of his panzer command, one of Hitler's adjutants arrived at Rundstedt's headquarters outside Paris. He presented Rundstedt with a coveted decoration, the oak leaves to his Knight's Cross, and a polite note from the Führer retiring the sixty-eight-year-old field marshal for reasons of age and health.

To replace him as commander in chief West, Hitler passed over Rommel and appointed Field Marshal Günther Hans von Kluge, an energetic sixty-one-year-old Prussian. Kluge, recently recovered from an auto accident in Russia where he had served as an army group commander, had spent the last fortnight at Berchtesgaden listening to Hitler blame faulty leadership for all the problems in Normandy. Consequently, in their first meeting, Kluge confronted Rommel with a catalog of the latter's purported shortcomings, including defeatism and disobedience. Rommel, who saw his new superior as another "eastern general" with no experience of Allied air power and other technical resources, fought back. He insisted that Kluge withdraw his insults and apologize in writing. The argument became so heated that Kluge cleared the room of aides so the two field marshals could harangue each other further. But Kluge afterward took a two-day tour of the front and came back with a new appreciation of his subordinate's

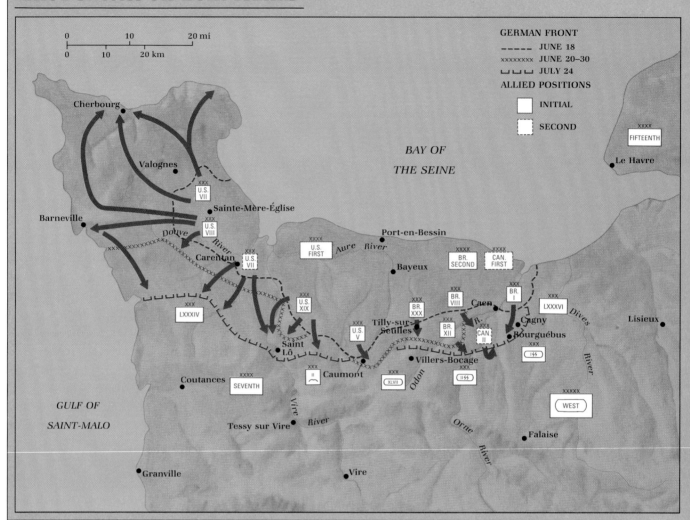

problems—and profuse apologies as balm to Rommel's wounded pride.

As the fighting against the British around Caen subsided again into stalemate, action flared up on the German left, which had been relatively quiet since the fall of Cherbourg. The American sector now extended westward for some fifty miles, from the salient around Caumont—where the American beachhead was nearly twenty miles deep—roughly westward to the Atlantic coast on the Gulf of Saint-Malo at the base of the Cotentin Peninsula. Deployed along this line were fourteen American divisions confronting six German divisions of the LXXXIV Corps, plus the 2d Paratroop Division of Hausser's Seventh Army. Half of the German divisions contained formations that had been drastically reduced in size. None had formidable armor, although they were well equipped with assault guns and divisional artillery. Four-fifths of the panzers in Normandy were concentrated in the eastern sector to contain a British breakthrough that might put enemy tanks in the rear of Rommel's forces.

On July 3, the day Kluge took command, the Americans launched their first full-scale offensive southward. It consisted of a series of three major assaults carried out over five days in corps strength and in echelon. The offensive was designed to reach the line formed by the three cities of Caumont, Saint-Lô, and Coutances. Success would straighten the front and

vastly enlarge the Allied beachhead, which now consisted of only one-fifth the area anticipated by the planners. Most important, the advance would take the Americans out of the marshlands, sunken roads, and hedgerows—the bocage that severely limited the mobility of their mechanized forces.

In the first thrust, on the German far left near the coast, the four divisions of the U.S. VIII Corps plunged into country laced with hedgerows and waterlogged by recent rains. There, they were quickly slowed to a crawl, not only by the difficult terrain but also by the stubborn resistance of the German fighting men. Hausser's defenders—soon to be augmented by the 15th Paratroop Regiment from Brittany and two battalions from the 2d SS Panzer Division—were ordinary German infantrymen, not the highly trained elite of Panzer Lehr or Meyer's young extremists of the 12th SS Panzer Division. But they fought with skill and tenacity. Indeed, postwar studies would indicate that in Normandy and other western battlegrounds, ordinary German soldiers like these outperformed their Allied opponents.

A number of explanations were offered to account for the apparent German superiority in combat. A British brigadier in Normandy asserted simply, "The Germans liked soldiering. We didn't." But there were more concrete reasons. German combat units tended to deploy a higher percentage of their strength in the front lines, rather than in supporting roles. German fighting units possessed superb leadership at the regimental level and below, and most were leavened by the presence of combat veterans. Moreover, the German army's tactical doctrine, and its training, encouraged initiative and flexibility in combat. German soldiers also had another motivation to fight hard—the powerful fear of what would happen if Germany lost the war. A German soldier who served in Normandy, Corporal Adolf Hohenstein of the 276th Infantry Division, recalled that he and his comrades were driven most of all by the Allied insistence on Germany's unconditional surrender. "If for the rest of my life I was to chop wood in Canada or Siberia," he said, "then I would sooner die in Normandy."

The combination of German tenacity and terrain that favored the defense stymied the American drive on Hausser's far left. In twelve days of the most difficult fighting, the U.S. VIII Corps advanced a mere seven miles—only one-third of the distance to its objective, Coutances—at a cost of 10,000 men killed, wounded, or captured.

Farther east, the Germans also largely thwarted the second American thrust southward. General Collins's VII Corps, the conquerors of Cherbourg, attempted to advance down the road from Carentan on July 4 and ran into the remnants of the 6th Paratroop Regiment and elements of the 17th SS Panzergrenadier Division. American casualties were so heavy on the first day that Lieut. Colonel Heydte, the officer who had risked a court martial by pulling his paratroopers out of Carentan three weeks previously, gallantly sent back captured American medics so that they could help evacuate the wounded. After eleven days of fighting during which his U.S. 4th Division suffered 2,300 casualties, Major General Raymond O. Barton reported, "The Germans are staying there just by the guts of their soldiers."

The third American attack encountered difficulties of a different kind. When the three infantry divisions of the newly committed U.S. XIX Corps jumped off on July 7, they found surprisingly light resistance. Rommel had already committed most of his reserves to meet the other threats. In the eleven-mile stretch between XIX Corps and its goal, the vital intersection of four national roads at Saint-Lô, Rommel had only Kampfgruppe Heinz, an improvised battle group consisting of three infantry battalions backed up by a reduced regiment from the 17th SS Panzergrenadiers. The Americans made such rapid progress the first day that the entire 3d Armored Division was soon brought up to cross the Vire River and finish the job. The result was a congestion of tanks and other vehicles on the narrow roads and in the adjacent hedgerows north of Saint-Lô so horrendous that the advance bogged down of its own weight.

Then, just as the Americans began to get unsnarled, the panzers struck. On July 9, a tank-infantry task force of the ubiquitous 2d SS Panzer Division stung the Americans at Le Désert, six miles northwest of Saint-Lô. Rommel, meanwhile, was preparing a much bigger blow. He had pulled the battle-hardened Panzer Lehr out of the Caen line the week before and placed it in reserve. Now, Fritz Bayerlein's panzers and truck-borne infantry were making a lateral move southward and westward behind the front, traveling so late at night to elude enemy planes that one tank commander played the harmonica in the vehicle's turret to keep his driver from dozing off.

On July 11, two columns from Panzer Lehr drove into American positions five miles north of Saint-Lô. Although the division had shrunk to one-third of its D-day strength and could field only thirty-two tanks, it had the advantage of overcast skies, which grounded Allied aircraft, and succeeded in penetrating up to two miles. Then, the skies cleared, and the planes came. On the ground, American gunners were on the defensive for a change and able to take advantage of the bocage to give the Germans a dose of their own antitank medicine. Lehr lost twenty panzers, and although it had temporarily checked the American advance on Saint-Lô, its surviving tanks and troops had to limp to the rear for reassignment farther west.

On that same day, the defenders of Saint-Lô faced a new threat. Yet another American corps joined the offensive. The U.S. V Corps, which had been guarding the quiet Caumont salient, pushed westward and captured a key hill only four miles east of Saint-Lô. Together with the XIX Corps from

After weeks of bombing from the air and shelling from the ground, the ancient city of Saint-Lô lies in pulverized ruin. German propagandists pointed to the lifeless city as an example of how the Americans and British were destroying France while liberating it.

the north, these Americans slowly pushed back the defensive force, which now consisted of three patched-together German battle groups from the LXXXIV Corps and the 3d Paratroop Division of General Eugen Meindl's II Paratroop Corps, which had been rushed over from the Caumont sector. The local commanders realized that a withdrawal was crucial. Despite Hitler's stand-fast doctrine, Hausser ordered Meindl to pull his troops back to the heights a mile south of Saint-Lô. Rommel's headquarters gave its tacit approval. "Just report to us afterward that the enemy penetrated your main line of resistance in several places and that you barely succeeded in reestablishing a new line to the rear," Rommel's commanders were told.

American troops faced only a rear guard when they fought their way into the ruined city on July 18. The capture of Saint-Lô ended the three-pronged offensive launched on July 3. In sixteen days of fighting, the three American corps had achieved their objectives only at Saint-Lô, and they had paid the price of more than 40,000 casualties.

The American offensive had forced Rommel to scramble ever more desperately to counter each new threat. From his headquarters at La Roche-Guyon, he raced to the front each morning. Despite the danger from the air, he covered as many as 400 miles a day in his efforts to find and galvanize the units to meet the rapidly shifting weight of the Allied attacks. Although his forces and the Allies had suffered roughly the same number of casualties—about 100,000 killed, wounded, or missing—the Americans and British were able to replace all their losses. Rommel, receiving replacements at a rate of less than 10 percent, was now outnumbered four to one in Normandy. And his supply situation was steadily worsening.

German paratroopers scurry between hedgerows to get into position to attack Allied tanks advancing on Saint-Lô. The lead man is carrying an 88-mm M 43 *Panzerschreck* (Tank Terror), a shoulder-fired weapon modeled after the U.S. Army's 2.36-inch bazooka.

In order to counter the American advance, Rommel had to give up his durable foothold in the British sector. Even before Panzer Lehr's failed counterattack in front of Saint-Lô, the British had taken advantage of that division's absence at Caen. Late on July 7—the same day the Americans launched their drive against Saint-Lô—a massive bombardment fell on the northern half of Caen. Allied artillerymen fired 80,000 shells; 460 four-engine craft from the RAF's Bomber Command unloaded some 2,500 tons of high explosives. Early the next morning, three British and Canadian divisions, supported by three armored brigades, attacked and found in Caen what one soldier described as "just a waste of brick and stone, like a field of corn that has been plowed."

The bombardment actually may have worked against the Allies. The artillery overshot most of the German defenders, who were dug in close to the British lines, and caused perhaps 5,000 French civilian casualties instead. In some places, the mountainous rubble and enormous craters impeded British progress through the city and provided improvised fortifications for the Germans. The battle raged from street to street. The inexperienced unit that had replaced Panzer Lehr, the 16th Luftwaffe Field Division, made up of air force ground personnel and flak crews converted to infantry, dissolved after suffering 75 percent casualties. Many teenagers of the 12th SS Panzer Division held on, fighting and dying among the ruins with a few flak guns and a handful of tanks, accounting for most of the 103 British tanks destroyed. On the western outskirts of Caen, Captain Ritzel, commander of the 1st Flak Battery of the 12th SS Flak Battalion, defended his position with his last remaining 88-mm, knocking out three British tanks before being overrun. Ritzel and his six crewmen still able to fight were all killed in hand-to-hand combat defending their gun pit.

The 12th Panzer's fervent commander, Kurt "Panzer" Meyer, finally gave way. Because he "just couldn't watch those youngsters being sacrificed to a senseless order," he defied Hitler's standing orders and evacuated his positions in Caen early on July 9. Later that day, the British gained control of the section of the city that lay north and west of the Orne River. After thirty-three days of trying, Field Marshal Montgomery had captured at least part of Caen. In the southern suburbs of the city, however, on the far bank of the Orne, his old rival Rommel had established a strong new line. Both commanders were now in trouble with their respective leaders: Rommel for his alleged defeatism, Montgomery for the failure to break out into the open plain that led beyond Caen.

Desperate to rectify this failure, Montgomery shifted his focus to the area northeast and east of Caen, where his troops had long maintained a bridgehead over the Orne. While a corps of Canadians drove into the

Colonel Hans von Luck, commander of a battle group in the 21st Panzer Division, (consulting the map at left) played a pivotal role in disrupting Operation Goodwood, the British offensive against Caen on July 18. Following a massive Allied air attack that blanketed the sky with smoke *(below)* and upturned several tanks, including the sixty-three-ton Tiger at right, Luck single-handedly organized a defense against the British ground assault.

southern half of Caen from the west as a diversion, he intended to launch three armored divisions in a swift strike southward from the bridgehead. The attack was code-named Goodwood, after an English racetrack. As a prelude early on the morning of July 18—the same day the Americans took Saint-Lô—an armada of more than 2,000 Allied warplanes poured some 8,000 tons of bombs on German positions. The heaviest aerial bombardment ever delivered against ground forces, it flung German Tiger tanks onto their sides, twisted flak guns on their mountings, and so stunned some defenders that they shook uncontrollably for hours.

Yet the bulk of the defenders emerged remarkably unscathed, and they were waiting when the British tanks moved out through the billowing smoke and dust at 7:30 a.m. Rommel had suspected the attack was coming. He had been alerted by prisoner-of-war interrogations and photographs from daring reconnaissance flights by the outnumbered Luftwaffe. He deployed his forces across the Allied axis of advance in a series of defensive belts nearly ten miles deep and composed of entrenched infantry backed by antitank and light artillery. Several miles south of Caen on Bourguébus Ridge, lay the main artillery support—more than 250 field and 88-mm guns as well as 272 five- and six-barreled Nebelwerfers. A few miles behind the ridge was a mobile reserve of some 80 big panzers and assault guns.

The vanguard of Montgomery's 700 tanks rolled easily south through the initial zone of bomb-decimated German infantry but ran into trouble at midmorning near the fortified hamlet of Cagny, three miles southeast of Caen and three miles northeast of Bourguébus. A German commander,

Colonel Hans von Luck, watching from an orchard at the edge of Cagny, saw the long columns of Shermans approaching northwest of town. Luck, a highly decorated thirty-three-year-old veteran of campaigns from Poland to Russia, had just returned early that morning from a three-day leave in Paris and was trying, from the 21st Panzer Division, to make radio contact with the battle group he commanded. All he could find in Cagny was one of the division's 88-mm antitank guns and a battery of four 88-mm flak guns. The battery belonged to the fragments of the 16th Luftwaffe Field Division that had survived two tremendous bombing raids in less than a fortnight, and the guns were still trained skyward.

Luck ordered the battery commander to move his guns to the edge of the orchard and take on the enemy tanks he had just seen. The Luftwaffe commander at first refused, insisting that his mission was air defense, but then complied after Luck drew his pistol. Rapidly redeployed in the orchard under Luck's command, the five 88s opened up against the procession of enemy tanks, firing into their thinly armored side plates. Sherman after Sherman—at least a dozen—burst into flame. Then, well into the afternoon, Luck mobilized the surviving tanks of his battle group, which were reinforced by antitank teams and six Tigers of the 503d Heavy Tank Battalion located east of the village. These random little forces destroyed dozens more tanks and successfully delayed the British advance, preventing much of Mongomery's armor from reaching its objective, Bourguébus Ridge, three miles to the southwest.

By late afternoon, Montgomery's armored strike had been severely disrupted not only by the superb German defense but by its own tactical shortcomings as well. As far back as the Orne bridgehead, scores of British tanks were still tangled in traffic jams created because the vehicles had to thread their way through narrow corridors in their own minefields.

The British spearhead, however, penetrated three of the German defensive zones and that afternoon neared the fourth, the 300-foot-high slopes of Bourguébus Ridge. There, nearly seven miles from their starting point and in tantalizing reach of the open plain to the south, the British had to contend with that fearsome array of antitank weapons—and then the panzers. Toward evening, the new German commander of Panzer Group West, General Hans Eberbach, launched a counterattack with four tank battalions of the 1st SS and 21st Panzer divisions. At dusk, the fifty-ton Panthers advanced against the British and shot up eighty of the lighter Shermans and Cromwells. But the counterattack soon ground to a halt against the mass of British armor.

The Germans held Bourguébus Ridge that night and for two more days against the British onslaught. By the time a violent thunderstorm turned

On the eve of the strafing attack that nearly killed him, Rommel *(right)* studies a map of Normandy with his chief of staff, General Hans Speidel. A member of the conspiracy to overthrow Hitler, Speidel encouraged Rommel to join the plotters.

the battlefield to mud and put an effective stop to Operation Goodwood on July 20, Rommel's men had destroyed or disabled more than 500 tanks—half of them on the first day. The total losses represented 36 percent of the British armored forces in Normandy. Although Montgomery's Canadian infantry had meanwhile completed the occupation of the ruins of Caen, the Germans had won an impressive defensive triumph by preventing the Allied breakout to the southeast.

For one last time, Rommel had stymied his old rival's armor—but he was not there to revel in the victory. In a Luftwaffe hospital forty miles east of Caen, the Desert Fox lay near death with multiple skull fractures and other severe injuries suffered three days previously on the eve of the battle. He had been returning to his headquarters from a last-minute visit to the I SS Panzer Corps headquarters when two British Typhoon fighter-bombers strafed his staff car, wounding the driver. The vehicle swerved into a tree and overturned, throwing Rommel onto the road. The accident occurred near a village with the sadly ironic name of Sainte-Foy-de-Montgomery.

The day of Rommel's last victory, July 20, a group of conspirators tried unsuccessfully to kill Hitler with a bomb. Rommel was not directly involved in the plot but had been aware of it. Some of the conspirators had hoped that, if the assassination succeeded, Rommel would agree to replace Hitler as chief of state and lead the Reich out of the war. Once the Führer learned this, the fate of the soldier he had once favored over all others was sealed. Rommel would slowly recover from his injuries during the next three months—then take poison rather than face trial for high treason. ✚

The Sweep to Germany's Doorstep

or nearly a week after the American capture of Saint-Lô on July 18, 1944, torrential rain and low clouds enforced a watchful lull on the Normandy front. While the Americans regrouped, General Paul Hausser, commander of the German Seventh Army, peppered his superiors with pleas for battlefield replacements, artillery, supplies, and, most of all, air cover. Hausser's army was in shreds. Once-cohesive fighting units were scattered along the twenty-five-mile stretch of road that ran southeast from Lessay, at the western base of the Cotentin Peninsula, through Périers, to the outskirts of Saint-Lô; in addition, they were virtually immobilized by lack of transport, equipment, weapons, and ammunition. Just west of Saint-Lô, between the Vire and the Taute rivers, Hausser had only about 5,000 combat-effective soldiers, nearly half of them from Lieut. General Fritz Bayerlein's elite Panzer Lehr Division. At full strength, Panzer Lehr was authorized 15,000 fighting men and 230 tanks and assault guns. After seven weeks of battle, the entire division could field scarcely 3,200 troops and a meager 50 or so armored vehicles.

Earlier in the month, Field Marshal Günther Hans von Kluge, the new commander in chief West, had extracted permission from Hitler to shift a total of four infantry divisions from southern France and from the Fifteenth Army still deployed at the Pas-de-Calais. But instead of sending the relief troops to Hausser, Kluge had used them to replace five armored divisions of General Hans Eberbach's Panzer Group West (reorganized as the Fifth Panzer Army on August 5), deployed opposite the British and Canadians near Caen. Kluge, recently ordered to take over for the injured Rommel as head of Army Group B in addition to his duties commanding OB West, hoped to give the panzer divisions a rest by converting them into a mobile reserve—a hope smashed by Field Marshal Sir Bernard Law Montgomery's launch of Operation Goodwood.

Kluge's preoccupation with protecting his right flank reflected the conviction held by the German high command that the primary Allied offensive would take place at the Pas-de-Calais. This obsession would effectively keep the Fifteenth Army at a distance from the fighting in Normandy—

His eyes shielded by goggles, a tank crewman of the 9th Panzer Division keeps a lookout from atop his camouflaged Panther for Allied fighter-bombers attacking out of the sun in August 1944. By month's end, all German forces in France, except those still holding isolated seaports, were in full retreat toward the German frontier.

leaving Hausser's Seventh Army and Eberbach's Panzer Group West to shoulder an immense burden as the sole defenders of the German left flank.

Shortly after noon on Monday, July 24, General Bayerlein answered a ringing telephone at Panzer Lehr headquarters in an old farmhouse in Canisy, located a few miles southwest of Saint-Lô. One of his regimental commands reported heavy bombing in front of the German lines. At one o'clock in the afternoon, American troops, who had withdrawn several hundred yards to the north just prior to the bombing, began to advance to their former positions.

The Germans did not know it, but the bombardment and ground offensive were a bad mistake—a false start to what was intended to be a major attack. Code-named Cobra, the strike had been meticulously planned by Lieut. General Omar N. Bradley and had originally been scheduled to take place on July 19, in order to take advantage of Operation Goodwood's launch. Poor weather had delayed Cobra until July 24, with the air attack set for noon. When the weather closed in again, the operation was called off—but not in sufficient time to stop a number of heavy bombers already en route to the target area.

The result was disaster. As the planes approached from the north, flying over the heads of American troops massed just north of the Saint-Lô-Périers road, bombs intended for the Germans began to fall short, a consequence of poor visibility and mechanical problems aboard some of the lead planes. The U.S. VII Corps's 30th Division, which was to initiate the ground attack, bore the brunt of the misguided bombing, losing 25 men killed and 131 wounded. In the aftermath of the botched effort, as the Americans assessed the damage and scrambled to reorganize for a second try the next day, Bradley was concerned that Cobra had lost the advantage of surprise. Incredibly, it had not.

Eyes still locked on Caen, Kluge was convinced that the next Allied move would be made by the British. That night, he shifted the 2d Panzer Division from near Caumont to the Orne River valley, west of Caen. Bayerlein, for his part, was gratified by the state of affairs at the end of the day. Although he disagreed with Kluge and fully expected the attack to recommence on his own front, he was confident that Panzer Lehr—which had, after all, prevented the Americans from crossing the Saint-Lô-Périers road—would again acquit itself well. Leaving only a light force north of the highway, he withdrew the bulk of his division to positions just south of the road. It was a decision the panzer commander would live to regret.

The fury from the sky on July 25 began at 9:38 a.m. "The planes kept coming over, as if on a conveyor belt," Bayerlein remembered afterward.

A column of German trucks goes up in smoke in a frame of footage taken from a strafing American fighter plane in July 1944. Lacking protection from the weakened Luftwaffe, the retreating Germans were easy targets for the Allied air forces.

"The bomb carpets unrolled in great rectangles. My flak had hardly opened its mouth when the batteries received direct hits that knocked out half the guns and silenced the rest."

More than 1,500 B-17s and B-24s, nearly 400 medium bombers, and approximately 550 fighter-bombers unloaded a total of 4,100 tons of bombs, high explosives, and napalm on the Cobra target—a doomed area located south of the Saint-Lô-Périers road measuring 7,000 yards wide by 2,500 yards deep. Within the hour, Bayerlein's communications had been destroyed; no command was possible. "By midday," he commented later, "the entire area resembled a moonscape, with the bomb craters touching rim to rim, and there was no longer any hope of getting out any of our weapons." The effect on his troops, Bayerlein said, was "indescribable." Three battalion command posts of Panzer Lehr had been destroyed, and

Taking cover behind a wrecked American tank that had been flipped on its side, a German artillery forward observer directs the fire of his battery against units of the U.S. First Army positioned near Saint-Lô.

Dull-eyed with shock from the devastating Allied bombing that accompanied Operation Cobra near Saint-Lô, soldiers of the German II Paratroop Corps wear tags identifying them as prisoners of war.

at least 70 percent of the men were "dead, wounded, crazed, or numbed."

Moving through the dust and smoke of the bombardment came the infantrymen of the U.S. 9th, 4th, and 30th divisions. Their immediate objective was to seal off the flanks of the bombed area to create a three-mile-wide corridor between Marigny and Saint-Gilles. Motorized troops would then drive southwest to Coutances and on to the Atlantic, to encircle the Germans facing the U.S. VIII Corps, mired in the bocage on the American right. To the south lay Brittany and the ports on the Atlantic coast, which the Allies needed for their logistical buildup and the funneling of supplies to their forces in the interior.

Despite all precautions, some of the Allied bombing had again taken an unintended toll of American troops. The men of the U.S. VII Corps were still reeling in shock as they began a hesitant advance—only to encounter stubborn remnants of Panzer Lehr. What many of the Americans had expected to be a cakewalk turned into the same slogging fight that had been going on since D-day. From networks of foxholes supported by a few tanks and 88-mm guns, Panzer Lehr slowed the Americans to a crawl.

Continued air attacks, however, frustrated German efforts to regroup and build a new line of defense. Tenacious as Panzer Lehr's strongpoints were, the Americans soon realized that the fortifications did not form a continuous belt and could be outflanked. By late afternoon, General Hausser counted seven penetrations of his line. By nightfall, the Americans had advanced from one to three miles beyond the morning's front. Field Marshal Kluge, who had rushed to Caen that day in response to an attack by

the Canadian II Corps, reported: "As of this moment, the front has burst."

The next day, although not all the intermediate objectives had been reached, Lieut. General J. Lawton "Lightning Joe" Collins, commander of the U.S. VII Corps, gambled and committed his armor. If Hausser had expected the terrain to come to the aid of his Seventh Army, he was in for a nasty surprise. The hedgerows had lost much of their defensive power: Aided by an ingenious adaptation—developed in strict secrecy over several weeks—American armor had acquired unprecedented maneuverability. Lengths of steel scrap salvaged from the German beach obstacles had been welded onto the tanks' noses like multipronged tusks. Propelled by the Shermans' powerful engines, the Rhinos, as these modified tanks were called, slashed through the hedgerows as if they were pasteboard, allowing the tanks to abandon the lethal confinement of the narrow roads and take off across the countryside.

As the Shermans bypassed German strongpoints, Allied fighter-bombers rained death on the outflanked defenders. By the evening of July 26, key road networks that would permit greater exploitation were under American control. The 1st Infantry Division had reached Marigny, astride a crossroads just north of the main road west to Coutances. To the east, Saint-Gilles was also firmly in American hands, and the troops of the 30th Division had moved south to Canisy, Panzer Lehr's division headquarters.

Torn-up track and splintered railroad cars at the Caen terminal on the Paris-Cherbourg line exemplify the damage that Allied bombers inflicted on German communications in France during July and August 1944. Denied supplies and reinforcements, the German Seventh Army could not prevent the Allied breakout from Normandy.

General Bayerlein had barely escaped to a temporary headquarters at Dangy, three miles farther south. That night, he gathered the ragged remains of his division: "I had fourteen tanks in all," he wrote later. "We could do nothing but retreat." Grimy and disheveled, Bayerlein received a visitor that evening—a staff officer from Kluge's headquarters. "Herr General," the officer began, "the field marshal demands that the line from Saint-Lô to Périers be held," adding that a battalion of SS Panther tanks had been dispatched to provide support.

Bayerlein could scarcely contain his fury. "Out in front, everyone is holding out," he replied grimly. "Everyone. My grenadiers and my engineers and my tank crews—they're all holding their ground. Not a single man is leaving his post. They are lying in their foxholes mute and silent, for they are dead. Dead. Do you understand? You may report to the field marshal that the Panzer Lehr Division is annihilated. Only the dead can now hold the line."

Kluge's demands that his subordinate commanders resist even as their positions were being overrun echoed the exhortations of the Führer: Throughout the fighting in Normandy, Hitler steadfastly refused suggestions to implement strategic withdrawals—until it was too late. That Kluge would not order withdrawals on his own responsibility may well have been an act of self-preservation. Since the failed July 20 attempt on Hitler's life, the Führer had grown increasingly suspicious of the higher ranks in the German army. Even though Kluge had played no part in the coup, he had been sympa-

Driving through a ravaged section of Falaise, members of a Luftwaffe ground unit scan the sky for enemy fighter-bombers. German soldiers in Normandy had to keep one eye on the sky at every moment of the day.

thetic to the cause and may have felt it prudent to demonstrate his loyalty.

Loyalty, prudent or otherwise, could not protect the German soldiers on the line. Kept under constant ground attack and hunted relentlessly from the air, the men of the Seventh Army were demoralized and exhausted. One German commander bivouacked his regiment under cover—hiding from friend and foe alike—to give them twenty-four hours of sleep. The strategy of the Allies—swinging their power alternately between Caen and Saint-Lô, maintaining the initiative, making it impossible for German divisions safely to leave one arena in order to reinforce the other—inflicted heavy punishment. Even as Kluge continued to give the Caen sector top priority, German soldiers around Saint-Lô were surrendering or fleeing southward.

The destruction of Panzer Lehr had left a yawning gap between General Dietrich von Choltitz's LXXXIV Corps on the German left and General Eugen Meindl's II Paratroop Corps on the right. The American Shermans charged through it. By the morning of July 28, Kluge knew he had to try to repair Hausser's disintegrating front. Hitler had released the 9th Panzer Division from southern France, but it would not reach Normandy for more than a week. Reluctantly, Kluge raided two panzer divisions from Eberbach's Panzer Group West and sent them to the Vire River just south of Saint-Lô, a piecemeal commitment that typified the German response in Normandy and would ultimately spell disaster.

That night, following a sharp skirmish with German rearguard troops, the U.S. VIII Corps, which had moved south from Périers, took Coutances. During the next two days, driven by the aggressive Lieut. General George S. Patton, the 4th Armored Division made dramatic gains in the direction of Avranches, gateway out of the Cotentin Peninsula into Brittany. Avranches lies on a 200-foot bluff between two westward-flowing rivers, the Sée to the north and the Sélune, some four miles to the south. From the north and east, five highways funnel across the Sée on two bridges. Only one main road leaves Avranches to the south, passing across the Sélune near Pontaubault. There, the highway splits like a crow's three-toed foot, heading east, south, and west.

The Germans needed to keep Avranches and the Pontaubault area in order to block a breakout into Brittany. But Hausser's forces were woefully outmanned and outgunned. Patton's 4th Armored Division entered an undefended Avranches on the evening of July 30, having unwittingly passed by the German Seventh Army's command post a few miles north of the town. Several generals, including Hausser himself, escaped through the American columns and fled east toward Mortain. The next day, the Americans captured their key objective: the bridge at Pontaubault. To their amazement, it was unscathed.

Upon learning of the fall of Avranches, Kluge signaled Colonel Rudolf Bacherer of the 77th Infantry Division that the town—the "keystone of our defense"—must be retaken and "held at all costs." Bacherer's division, hard hit during July, had been sent to the Pontaubault area south of Avranches for a rest. Although the 77th was in poor shape to face the Allied might on its own, Colonel Bacherer was resourceful. He rounded up fourteen self-propelled guns and an assortment of stragglers, as well as units of the 5th Paratroop Division. With that makeshift band, Bacherer performed remarkably well: Fighting under a drizzling sky that kept the planes away, he retook Pontaubault, house by house.

Then, the skies cleared, and the fighter-bombers arrived. As the bulk of his ragtag force retreated, Bacherer dispatched demolition parties to blow up the Pontaubault Bridge. But the sappers never made it past the American tanks and infantry. In the end, Bacherer was forced to leave the bridge intact. Not even the Luftwaffe, despite several attempts during the next week, could destroy it.

The German defenses on the Cotentin Peninsula had crumbled. On the last day of July, the U.S. 4th and 6th Armored divisions took more than 4,000 prisoners, with another 3,000 scooped up by the supporting infantry divisions that were following behind. Fighter-bombers continued to attack the retreating Germans, and charred vehicles and abandoned equipment choked the roads, slowing their retreat.

Thus, as August began, the Americans were poised to burst into Brittany. As of noon on August 1, George Patton became head of the newly operational U.S. Third Army, and he wasted no time leading his force into battle. (Third Army—along with First Army, now headed by Lieut. General Courtney H. Hodges—had become part of the U.S. Twelfth Army Group, under Bradley.) With fighter-bombers and antiaircraft guns throwing up a protective air umbrella, Patton—the man whom Hitler called "that crazy cowboy general"—whipped seven divisions (more than 100,000 men and 15,000 vehicles) across the Sélune in seventy-two hours. As the 6th Armored Division drove west toward Brest and the 4th headed southwest for Lorient and Saint-Nazaire, they faced only disorganized German units scrambling for their lives into the fortified Breton ports.

The Third Army gobbled up the French countryside. Yet by the conventional standards of warfare, Patton was dangerously overexposed. Behind him to the north and east stretched a fragile line of communications. At his headquarters in East Prussia, poring over maps of the battle in France, Hitler looked at the lengthening Allied columns and decided to attack. "We must strike like lightning," he told his staff on August 2. "When we reach the sea, the American spearheads will be cut off." The Führer refused to worry about Patton's forces racing through Brittany—"Their turn will come later." Hitler's plan, Operation Lüttich, would be the last great counteroffensive effort in the Normandy campaign.

The plan called for Kluge to thrust eight of the nine panzer divisions in Normandy from Mortain toward Avranches in a drive to the sea that would then turn north to destroy the Allied beachhead. Hitler believed that such a full-blooded counterattack was a "unique, never recurring opportunity for a complete reversal of the situation."

Kluge and Hausser were appalled at Hitler's idea. Kluge, who thought the generals at OKW were "living on the moon," favored retaking Avranches, but only to anchor a new line of defense. If Hitler's massive counterthrust failed, the commander in chief West feared that an orderly withdrawal to defensive positions on the Seine would be difficult—perhaps impossible.

Still, if he had to carry out Hitler's order, Kluge wanted to act quickly, before the American envelopment cut off his movement entirely. Because assembling eight divisions would take far too long, he devised a plan that would use the four panzer divisions already in the area—the 2d, 116th, 1st SS Leibstandarte Adolf Hitler, and 2d SS. Three of them would penetrate

Burning trucks of the 21st Panzer Division clog the highway near Mont Pinçon, twenty-five miles northwest of Falaise. The convoy had been hit by Allied planes flying cover for the British Second Army.

Smoke roils skyward from the wreckage of a panzer destroyed by a Canadian tank (far left) near Falaise in August 1944. The fighting in the Falaise pocket was the largest clash of armor on the western front: ten Allied tank divisions facing ten German panzer divisions—two fewer than the Germans had deployed against the Soviets during the battle for Kursk in 1943.

near Mortain, and the fourth would pass through, down the valley of the Sée River, to capture Avranches. Hitler protested that Kluge's reduced force, composed of only 250 tanks, would be too weak to accomplish his grand objectives. But in the end, he agreed to let the strike go forward.

Operation Lüttich was doomed from the start. Thanks again to the code-cracking capabilities of Ultra, the Allies had been monitoring communications between OB West and OKW, and Bradley was ready. Four American divisions—the 3d Armored, the battle-hardened 30th and 4th, with the 2d Armored in support—were assigned to block Kluge's path to the ocean. The scheme dovetailed with a major change to the original invasion plan. Instead of trying to capture the Breton ports, the Allies would capitalize on the collapsing German resistance. The new plan called for Patton to use minimum force in clearing Brittany while sending most of the Third Army in a sweeping drive to the east. Meanwhile, General Hodges's First Army would continue the pressure in the area between Vire and Mortain, wheeling northeastward even as the Canadians pressed toward Falaise and the British attacked Argentan. The intent was to envelop Kluge's forces west of the Seine or, if that attempt failed, to crush them

By mid-August, retreat was the only salvation for the Germans fighting in Normandy. The haggard group shown below is hiding from Allied planes in a forest near Falaise. Tens of thousands of other soldiers were either killed, like the dead SS sergeant *(left)* lying beside a wrecked armored vehicle, or captured, like the bloody-faced panzergrenadier *(opposite)*.

against the river. As Bradley told a visitor to the front, "This is an opportunity that comes to a commander not more than once in a century. We are about to destroy an entire German army."

At midnight on August 6, the vanguard of the 2d SS Panzer advanced on the north side of Mortain and overran outposts of the U.S. 30th Division before being stopped by infantry and an antitank battalion equipped with assault weapons. Fourteen German tanks were destroyed. The 2d Panzer Division, moving along the south bank of the Sée River, made it halfway to Avranches before being halted by Allied fighters; the advance of the experienced 1st SS Panzer barely got started before being stopped in its tracks by the U.S. 3d Armored Division.

At dawn, the U.S. 2d Armored Division counterattacked. With help from Thunderbolts of the British Second Tactical Air Force, which flew 294 sorties that day, the Americans shredded 2d Panzer's tank strength to thirty. The German commanders on the ground looked for their own protective air umbrella—in vain. Luftwaffe aircraft had in fact taken off from Paris, but no sooner were they airborne than they were attacked above their bases by Allied fighters. Not one of them reached the battlefields near Avranches.

By midafternoon of August 7, Kluge was ready to disengage. Instead, a furious Hitler ordered him to bring in more panzers and renew the offensive, setting August 9 as the target date. Kluge was incredulous. "The attack on Avranches will result in the complete collapse of the whole Normandy front," he forecast to General Hans Eberbach, whose Fifth Panzer Army was to hold a defensive line farther north, near Falaise.

As Kluge and Hausser reluctantly prepared to follow Hitler's orders, Montgomery launched his drive toward Falaise. The Allies called it Operation Totalize. Two armored divisions of the Canadian First Army led the attack, following a midnight carpet bombing almost as massive as the one dropped for the launch of Cobra. Despite the pummeling, the German ground forces fought back with such determination that after two days of costly combat, Montgomery called a halt. Totalize had not reached its objective, but Allied armor was now in position to threaten the German forces in Normandy from the rear.

The German success at Falaise was both temporary and exceptional.

Hausser's Seventh Army and Eberbach's Fifth Panzer Army were in disarray. The surviving infantry was in tatters, as were the armored divisions. "Condition of these straggling sections mostly very bad," Hausser noted in a report to Kluge. "Many without headgear, without belts, and with worn footwear. Many go barefoot." Lacking supplies and forced to live off the countryside, the Germans also had to deal with vengeful French civilians. "Hatred and terrorist activity are intensified," Hausser wrote, blaming "enemy command of the air" for the appalling state of his troops.

The Germans were in imminent danger of being trapped. Despite fierce resistance, Montgomery's Twenty-first Army Group was forging south to cut off the German line of retreat to the Seine, while Bradley's Twelfth Army Group—in the form of Patton's racing Third Army—was swinging north to meet it. Meanwhile, Allied pounding from the air never abated. The roads were clogged with smashed German supply columns and fleeing troops. "On August 13," wrote a German soldier, "I lost everything but my life and the rags on my back."

Still the Germans fought on. In Falaise, sixty teenagers from the 12th SS Panzer Division holed up in a schoolhouse; for three days, they held off an overwhelming Canadian force. On August 17, the Canadians finally occupied the schoolhouse. They found fifty-six of the defenders dead, the remaining four wounded.

Two days earlier, with the noose drawing ever tighter around his beleaguered troops and Hitler still refusing to consider a withdrawal, Kluge had set out to inspect the battlefield. His staff car was strafed by Allied aircraft, and he was without communications for several hours. It was nearly midnight before he got back to his headquarters. Ever suspicious, Hitler concluded that Kluge's disappearance signaled that the field marshal had gone over to the enemy, and he determined to relieve Kluge of his command. On August 17, Field Marshal Walther Model arrived from the eastern front to replace Kluge as commander in chief West as well as commander of Army Group B.

The next day, Kluge bade his staff a somber farewell and set off by car for Germany, where he fully expected to be arrested by the Gestapo. Between Verdun and Metz, the field marshal killed himself by biting into a potassium cyanide capsule.

In one of his final orders, Kluge had risked Hitler's wrath and ordered Hausser to evacuate the German Seventh Army motor transport and administrative troops. But he would go no further toward a full retreat. As it happened, Model, a favorite of the Führer's, recognized the severity of the danger and ordered a withdrawal of the forces without consulting Hitler. By that time, however, the one escape route in the deadly pocket had

On July 25, the Americans broke through the overextended lines of the German Seventh Army west of Saint-Lô, destroying a large part of the German LXXXIV Corps at Tessy-sur-Vire and forcing Kluge to transfer two of his remaining panzer divisions westward to stem the Allied advance. On August 6, Kluge launched a powerful but unsuccessful counterattack in the area of Mortain. Meanwhile, Lieut. General Omar N. Bradley of the U.S. First Army sent two armored corps sweeping around to the south. By August 13, the Allies had nearly encircled the remnants of Hausser's Seventh Army and SS General Sepp Dietrich's Fifth Panzer Army in the vicinity of Falaise. While much of the German armor escaped through a gap near Argentan, 50,000 Germans surrendered, and some 10,000 were killed in the Falaise pocket

The Allied Encirclement at Falaise

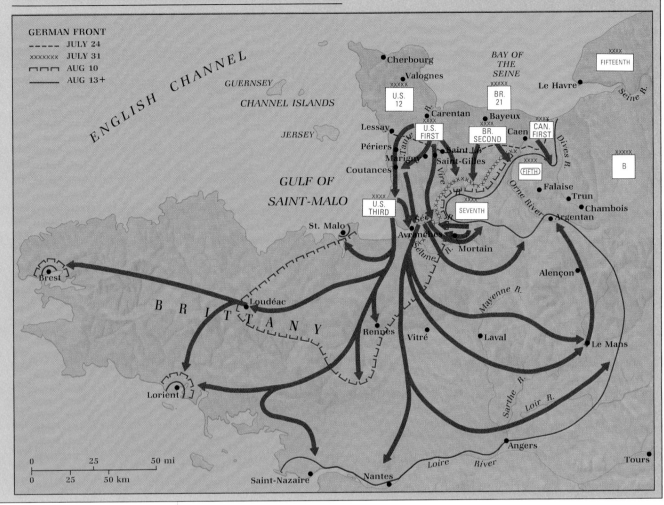

GERMAN FRONT
- - - - - JULY 24
xxxxxx JULY 31
⊓⊓⊓ AUG 10
――――― AUG 13+

ENGLISH CHANNEL

GUERNSEY
CHANNEL ISLANDS

JERSEY

GULF OF
SAINT-MALO

BRITTANY

Cherbourg
Valognes
BAY OF THE SEINE
Le Havre
U.S. 12
BR. 21
FIFTEENTH
Carentan
Bayeux
Lessay
U.S. FIRST
BR. SECOND
Caen
CAN. FIRST
Périers
Saint-Lô
Marigny
Saint-Gilles
Coutances
FIFTH
Falaise
Trun
U.S. THIRD
SEVENTH
Orne River
Argentan
Chambois
St. Malo
Avranches
Mortain
Dives R.
Seine R.
B
Brest
Alençon
Loudéac
Mayenne R.
Rennes
Vitré
Laval
Le Mans
Lorient
Sarthe R.
Loir R.
Angers
Nantes
Loire River
Tours
Saint-Nazaire

0   25   50 mi
0   25   50 km

shrunk from being twenty miles wide near Falaise to only six miles across, between the towns of Trun and Chambois.

On August 19, the gap narrowed as the two arms of the Allied pincers—the Canadian Second Army from the north and the U.S. Third Army from the south—approached Chambois. Trapped inside the pocket were 100,000 German soldiers, remnants of two armies and four corps. In a desperate move, Hausser ordered all units still capable of movement to "break out independently," as one of his generals put it, in headlong flight to the east. Their goal was a three-mile-long stretch of the Dives River between Trun and Chambois. Hampered by roads jammed with the wreckage of motorized vehicles and horse-drawn transport, the Germans made easy prey for Allied artillery and fighter planes. The slaughter was appalling. "My comrades died like flies," wrote one German soldier. "God grant that we come out of this alive." An American on the scene a few days later said it looked "as if an avenging angel had swept the area bent on destroying all things German."

The German commanders rallied their troops as best they could. Hausser and General Eugen Meindl of the II Paratroop Corps managed to lead 4,000 men, along with a considerable number of tanks and trucks, across the Dives. The 12th SS Panzer's indestructible commander, Kurt Meyer, also made it, swimming for his life through water that was choked with the bloated bodies of dead men and horses. With him came about 200 soldiers, all that remained of his division. After the crossing, Meyer remembered later, he "turned and cursed those who had senselessly sacrificed two German armies."

Between 20,000 and 40,000 men escaped from the Falaise pocket. Fully 60,000 had been left behind—killed, wounded, or captured. Proud divisions such as Panzer Lehr and the 12th SS Panzer survived in name only.

In the midst of the chaos, the survivors retained their discipline. Near Orville, ten miles east of the Dives, Meindl was asked by one of his officers, "What now?" He replied simply: "The Seine." Reforming and moving out in remarkable order, the II Paratroop Corps made it to the Seine at Louviers. Others managed to assemble near Rouen.

Hitler's vision of repelling the enemy at the Seine, however, was a fading illusion. The Germans had no fortified positions, no artillery, and no fresh, trained troops. Moreover, even before the survivors from Falaise reached the riverbank, Patton and his armor had control of the river just northwest of Paris. Soon, the Americans were crossing at Mantes. Another spearhead of Patton's army, slowed at first by a battle in Chartres—which, remarkably, had left the town's famed cathedral untouched—stood at Troyes, located 100 miles southeast of Paris.

As General Dwight D. Eisenhower traveled with the stream of Allied troops toward the French capital a few days after the Falaise gap was closed, he went through the killing ground near Chambois. There, he paused to regard the metal monuments to war—the smashed tanks, caissons, and artillery pieces that obstructed the narrow road running through the town. More appalling was the human carnage. "It was literally possible to walk for hundreds of yards at a time, stepping on nothing but dead and decaying flesh," the Allied supreme commander wrote. At Chambois, he heard Radio Berlin proclaim Falaise a noble achievement of German arms.

The costly defeat in Normandy was already irreversible when a second Allied invasion—another demonstration of the enemy's seemingly unlimited supplies of matériel and manpower—dealt a final blow to the Wehrmacht in France. Operation Dragoon, originally named Anvil, was first planned to take place on the French Riviera simultaneously with Operation Overlord in Normandy. But the lack of sufficient transport to mount a second landing caused Eisenhower to delay it for more than two months. The British would have preferred to cancel the operation altogether and use the resources to support the campaign in Italy. But the Americans argued that the capture of the port of Marseilles was vital for the support of operations in western Europe. Furthermore, at the Tehran Conference

Racing to Reach the Seine

On August 19 and 20, 1944, an estimated 20,000 to 40,000 German soldiers broke out of the Falaise pocket and raced pell-mell for the Seine River, seventy miles to the northeast, where the German high command hoped to form a new front on the river's east bank. Although thousands of the fleeing men were overrun by pursuing Allied columns and thousands more were killed by Allied planes, a German rear guard, organized by SS General Sepp Dietrich, prevented the retreat from becoming a rout.

As the beaten troops poured into the crossing sites in the area around Rouen, German engineers hastily assembled pontoon bridges, organized fleets of ferries, and rounded up anything else that would float. Some of the soldiers crossed the river on rafts made of barrels taken from nearby farms and on logs lashed together with telephone wire. Still others had to swim for it. By August 27, the Germans had moved most of the men to the opposite bank.

Rainy weather helped the Germans gain the badly needed reprieve by limiting the Allied onslaught from the air. Nevertheless, the Germans had to abandon nearly all of their tanks, guns, trucks, and half-tracks. "From the point of view of equipment abandoned," Sepp Dietrich later said, "the Seine crossing was almost as great a disaster as the Falaise pocket."

Heading for the Seine River, German soldiers escaping from the Falaise pocket ride a Tiger tank through the village of Bourgtheroulde, fourteen miles southwest of Rouen.

The Desperate Flight for Survival

German soldiers in a motorized assault boat prepare to tow a makeshift raft carrying a staff car across the Seine. Their comrades, stripped to their shorts, are steadying the car to prevent it from tipping into the water.

German soldiers in a motorized assault boat prepare to tow a makeshift raft carrying a staff car across the Seine. Their comrades, stripped to their shorts, are steadying the car to prevent it from tipping into the water.

Hoping to hitch a ride on a retreating vehicle, two SS panzergrenadiers stand in a square in Bourgtheroulde, close to a statue of a French World War I soldier. One of the road signs points out an assembly area for the sick.

The shattered hulks of an 88-mm gun and two half-tracks (*opposite*) lie amid the rubble on the docks at Rouen after the Germans had escaped.

in November 1943, the Allies had promised Stalin that they would invade southern France, and American president Franklin D. Roosevelt did not want to break his word. Although Churchill protested to the end, the Americans prevailed, and the second D-day was set for August 15.

The German high command had been expecting such an attack since the previous winter and had beefed up their shore fortifications accordingly. But manpower and armor were another matter. With the Allied breakout from Normandy, a south-to-north transfusion of troops began. By the end of July, General Johannes Blaskowitz, commander of Army Group G— consisting largely of the Nineteenth Army—had lost both the 2d SS and the 9th Panzer divisions to Army Group B in northern France, leaving only the 11th Panzer Division in reserve in the south. Once celebrated as the "Ghost" Division for its speed and aggressiveness, the 11th Panzer had been severely depleted on the eastern front and was in the process of rebuilding. By early August, it was scarcely at half-strength, possessing twenty-five Panzer IV and fifty Panzer V tanks; except for a core of veterans, its 12,000 troops were largely inexperienced. In any event, Blaskowitz had no control over the 11th Panzer; Hitler kept the division under OKW command, and only he could order it into action.

Along the Mediterranean coast, Blaskowitz and Nineteenth Army commander General Friedrich Wiese could count on 34,000 infantrymen, divided among eight divisions that were in varying states of readiness. One division had been badly mauled in Normandy, another severely punished in Russia. Yet a third was primarily used for training. Another 170,000 troops were stationed within a few days' march of the coastline. So stretched were the Reich's replacement resources that the Nineteenth Army's formations were filled with many men almost forty years old, a few young recruits, and prisoner-of-war conscripts from the eastern front whose loyalty was doubtful. Finally, Blaskowitz had one other reserve division, the 157th, which was at full strength but was quartered near Grenoble, 150 miles northeast of the probable invasion area, without enough motor transport to move quickly.

In July, the Allies intensified an air campaign that had begun in April to keep the Germans guessing as to where the invasion would come. In the course of those three months, Allied aircraft flew some 6,000 bombing sorties, striking as far inland as Lyons against roads, bridges, and ammunition dumps. Five of the six major railroad bridges over the Rhone, from Lyons south to the Mediterranean, were destroyed; and all double-line railroad track between Lyons and Avignon was cut in at least two places. Then, in the last five days before Operation Dragoon's launch, Allied strategic and tactical aircraft plastered the Riviera coast with bombs, flying more than 1,000 sorties a day and striking from Sète to Genoa in Italy. As in Normandy, the German air response was virtually nil. The 2d Air Division, responsible for the French Mediterranean, possessed at most 130 planes. These, along with aircraft in other commands in southwest France and Italy, gave the Germans a total of fewer than 250 serviceable planes, leading British Air Marshal Sir John Slessor to conclude that the Luftwaffe "could virtually be ignored."

On the water as in the air, Hitler's forces were sorely outmatched. One eight-hour-long air strike at Toulon on August 6 smashed 4 of only 7 remaining U-boats there, leaving 3 submarines, a destroyer, and some smaller craft to contend with an Allied amphibious force made up of 880

American troops herd German prisoners captured during the initial phase of Operation Dragoon past empty landing craft lining a beach on the French Riviera. In the absence of strong German coastal defenses, the American and French forces advanced quickly inland.

vessels and 1,370 landing craft. With staggering defeats already occurring on three fronts—in Normandy, the Soviet Union, and Italy—German prospects for repelling a fresh invasion were dim.

On August 15—Napoleon's birthday—some 9,000 Allied paratroopers drifted to earth in three drop zones near Le Muy, twelve miles inland from the invasion beaches, at the juncture of highways from Toulon, Cannes, and Avignon. Meanwhile, near Toulon, a squadron of six Allied planes sowed confusion among the Germans by dropping 500 parachute-borne dummies equipped with noisemakers that sounded like small arms fire. Preceded by predawn commando raids on Cap Negi and Île de Port-Cros

Like a flock of oversize birds, American gliders occupy a vineyard near Le Muy, twelve miles from the Cannes beaches. During the predawn hours of August 15, the gliders landed members of the U.S. 1st Airborne Task Force, who were to seize a critical road junction nearby.

on the left flank of the invasion, amphibious landings began at a half-dozen beach areas stretching from Cavalaire on the Allied western flank to Saint-Raphaël, near Cannes, in the east.

Although the Germans had guessed approximately where and knew exactly when the assault would occur, they could do little about it. Spread thinly along the seventy-mile stretch of coast, Blaskowitz could muster a front line of perhaps 12,000 troops to confront an initial invasion force roughly six times stronger. All hope for mounting a defense rested on the 11th Panzer, but OKW did not order that division to begin moving east of the Rhone from its station near Toulouse until August 13. Slowed by Allied air attacks, bombed-out bridges, and harassment by the French Resistance, the 11th Panzer was not in a position to be of use when the assault came.

Outnumbered and outgunned, the Germans in the south of France did the best they could. At Cavalaire Bay, they met oncoming enemy troops with machine guns and small arms; in less than an hour, withering fire from superior numbers drove them off the beach. At Saint-Tropez and near Sainte-Maxime, the story was essentially the same: The Germans inflicted what casualties they could and then retreated.

Eleven hundred miles northeast of the Provençal beaches, the mood at Hitler's headquarters in East Prussia was grim. General Alfred Jodl, chief of the operations staff for the armed forces high command, was struck by the "Führer's haggard look and his air of overwhelming distress." With Operation Dragoon scarcely six hours old, the German outlook was dismal. As dispatches from the front were rushed into Hitler's presence, each bearing more bad news, Hitler's staff waited for him to fly into one of his customary rages. Instead, the Führer became increasingly apathetic and indecisive. Finally, as the meeting broke up, he told Jodl that he would "consider the measures to be adopted in the eventuality that the situation in France should become unfavorable."

The situation deteriorated rapidly. By August 17, the Allies had put ashore more than 86,000 soldiers (of an eventual 380,000 total), 12,000 vehicles, and 46,000 tons of supplies. Some of the units had faced so little resistance after landing that they had penetrated as far as fifteen miles inland—a distance it had taken the Allies in Normandy two weeks to achieve. At this point, Hitler issued orders for a full-scale evacuation of the Wehrmacht from southern France.

The American forces moved farther inland, pushing north and west to get in position to cut off a German retreat up the Rhone Valley. Meanwhile, Free French forces under General Jean de Lattre de Tassigny had begun to come ashore. The French mission was to capture Toulon and Marseilles, then follow as quickly as possible up the west bank of the Rhone. An Allied

advance up the Rhone Valley could join with the forces that had broken out of Normandy and, in the process, bag the German Nineteenth Army.

Toulon and Marseilles were not easily won. Even as he ordered his armies to retreat, the Führer had made a familiar demand: The ports were to be held "to the last man." Those orders were taken to heart by the embattled and isolated garrisons. Elements of the 244th Infantry Division at Marseilles, led by Major General Hans Schaeffer, fought tenaciously, making good use of various barriers, including fortified islands just off-shore, a network of roadblocks, and antitank mines strung through the city's suburbs. For two weeks, the 244th absorbed the attacks of Free French forces and hung on through bombardments by the American battleship *Nevada* and by medium bombers from the U.S. Twelfth Air Force. But tenacity was not enough: By August 27, the few Germans still fighting were penned up in the Marseilles dock area; the following day, they surrendered.

As the bulk of the Nineteenth Army withdrew from the coastal region, its troops fought the biggest battle of the retreat at a narrow gorge called the Gate of Montélimar, about forty miles north of Avignon. There, the 11th Panzer Division and elements of the 198th and 338th Infantry divisions held open the escape route for eight days. At one point, a company of German infantry, accompanied by a handful of panzers, made a diversionary attack at Bonlieu, situated on one of the Rhone's tributaries. The diversion allowed a battalion of the 198th Division, supported by six Tiger tanks, to break through the American line farther north. Before the Allies could repair the breach, a considerable number of retreating Germans had filtered through. Not until August 28 did the U.S. VI Corps manage to block the Rhone escape route. By that date, however, they had already captured 57,000 German troops.

A few days before the Allies gained control of port facilities in the south, they won a prize in the north that they had, in fact, been trying to avoid: Paris. The French capital had not been one of Eisenhower's immediate objectives, for several tactical reasons. A direct attack would delay vigorous pursuit of the Seventh and Fifth Panzer armies. Liberation would saddle Eisenhower with two million Parisians in dire need of relief supplies. And finally, there were political ramifications. Eisenhower had no wish to intervene in the power struggle between the French political left and right. But if he enabled General Charles de Gaulle, de facto head of the French government-in-exile, to make a triumphant entrance into Paris, intervention was unavoidable.

The Allied supreme commander had thus planned to bypass and encircle the capital, isolating the German garrison located inside the city and

French policemen armed with captured rifles search for Germans in the rubble of an armory near the port city of Toulon on August 24, 1944. Shells fired by an Allied destroyer in the Mediterranean smashed the building, killing more than half of the 400 Germans inside, including the soldier in the foreground.

merely waiting for it to surrender. The bulk of Allied troops would keep on moving, using precious gasoline to reach their main goal—a bridgehead over the Rhine River—before winter set in. As General Bradley assessed the situation, Paris should have been "nothing more than an ink spot on our maps." But events took their own course, and in the end, the Allies felt

A German naval antiaircraft unit on the lower Seine at Rouen searches the skies for Allied fighter-bombers. Rouen was the Germans' last major foothold in France and a valuable inland harbor, serving as a prime transhipment point between seagoing vessels from the English Channel and river-going vessels headed for Paris.

compelled to liberate the City of Light, if only to save it from destruction.

As it happened, the city's true savior was an unlikely one: General Dietrich von Choltitz, who had been the commander of the LXXXIV Corps on the Cotentin Peninsula. In early August, at about the time Hitler was ordering Kluge to mount the counterattack at Mortain, the Führer appointed Choltitz to the new post of commanding general and military commander of Greater Paris. Among other things, Choltitz was charged with restoring discipline to troops who had become accustomed to an easy life far from the front and with keeping the civilian population in hand. Of utmost priority, however, was his mission to deny Paris to the enemy.

A Prussian careerist, Choltitz had taken part in the bloody siege of Sevastopol and later had led a division fighting in the rear guard of the German armies withdrawing from the Ukraine, faithfully executing Hitler's scorched earth policy. "It has been my fate," Choltitz once remarked, "to cover the retreat of our armies and to destroy the cities behind them." In light of this history of unquestioning obedience, the general's conduct in Paris was extraordinary.

Called to Hitler's headquarters in East Prussia from the crumbling front in Normandy, Choltitz had hoped to be inspired, as he had been by his first encounter with the Führer the year before. He had come, as he recalled later, "to be convinced again, to be assured that there was still a chance to change the course of the war."

The outcome was much different. A trembling Hitler spoke in an aimless

The bodies of German soldiers lie along the sidewalk in Rouen, close to a burning vehicle and some shattered trees. The Canadian First Army liberated the city on August 30, 1944.

whisper at first, and then he turned up the volume, shouting wildly about the new weapons that would reverse the tide in Normandy. Finally calming, he ordered Choltitz to rule Paris as though it were under siege, and to "stamp out without pity" any uprisings or acts of sabotage. Choltitz left the meeting not reinvigorated but shaken and full of doubt. "I was simply appalled," he wrote later, as he wondered whether Hitler had gone mad.

As Choltitz took up his new office, Eisenhower was concentrating on the breakout from Normandy and the subsequent sweep toward Germany. Word of Allied victories filtered back to occupied Paris, stirring elements of the political left and right to open rebellion. If two million Parisians decided to rebel, Choltitz and his small garrison of 5,000 soldiers would have more than they could handle.

On August 10, a Communist-led strike in a rail yard escalated quickly; within a few days, all train traffic in and out of Paris was cut. It was the first large-scale strike since the beginning of the German occupation in 1940, and as the agitation spread, Choltitz ordered that the Paris police be disarmed. His garrison was carrying out the order when virtually the entire 20,000-member police force went on strike. On August 15, with the metro no longer running and few people going to their jobs, crowds gathered outside Notre Dame Cathedral heard news of the invasion of southern France, and the ranks of the Resistance swelled.

Throughout the days of turmoil, Choltitz confined himself to issuing futile warnings to the citizens of Paris even as he was receiving, and

resisting, a stream of orders to demolish the city. On August 14, Field Marshal Kluge's chief of staff at OB West, General Günther Blumentritt, had passed on OKW's instructions to carry out a "limited scorched-earth policy" by wrecking the city's public utilities and selectively sabotaging its industrial plants. The first phase was to start at once.

Choltitz declined to carry out the order, pointing out that, at least for the time being, Paris's public utilities were as vital to the occupying forces as they were to the Parisians. Next came inquiries from Jodl, OKW's chief of operations. OKW had sent a team of demolition experts, led by Captain Werner Ebernach, to mine every bridge across the Seine. Now the Führer

After inspecting troops of the 2d Armored Division, General Charles de Gaulle *(center, right)*, accompanied by General Jacques Leclerc *(center)*, heads for the start of the grand victory parade on August 26, 1944, one day after the liberation of Paris. The march down the Champs Élysées celebrated the end of four years of German occupation.

wanted a report. Choltitz told Jodl that the preparations for mining were not yet finished and repeated the arguments against destroying the city that he had used with Blumentritt. Jodl warned that Hitler would not change his orders, but Choltitz had won a temporary reprieve.

As the military commander of Greater Paris stalled for time, Ebernach and his team went on with their demolition work, planting dynamite everywhere. With an ominous "sea of red crosses" spreading on the maps that Ebernach laid before him, Choltitz was well aware that the splendid city was living on borrowed time. Then, on the night of August 17, he was shown instructions signed by Kluge that day, just before he was relieved of command: "I give the order for the neutralizations and destructions envisaged for Paris."

Incredibly, Choltitz still did not act, not even when confronted that night by Field Marshal Model, Kluge's successor. He told Model that blowing up Paris would enrage its inhabitants and make defense against an Allied attack impossible. Model agreed to further delay, although in the end he said to Choltitz: "When we are finished, this city will be destroyed."

On August 19, as the Canadians and Americans closed the Falaise pocket, a full-scale insurrection broke out in the French capital. Members of the burgeoning Resistance, shooting and hurling Molotov cocktails, set aflame several of the panzers remaining in the city. The Germans answered with machine-gun fire and heavy fighting erupted near the Jardin du Luxembourg. At least 50 members of Choltitz's small garrison were killed and 100 wounded. The battle-hardened general concentrated his men in strongholds placed throughout the city.

Then Choltitz negotiated a deal. Approached by the Swedish consul general and Red Cross representative Raoul Nordling on August 20, he assented to a cease-fire—although he instructed the diplomat not to "associate my name with your truce." Just the day before, Choltitz had made another conciliatory gesture, agreeing to the release of 4,213 French prisoners held by the Germans. Now, he followed up with an even more dramatic grant of freedom. He set at liberty a pro-de Gaulle leader of the Resistance, Alexander Parodi.

Choltitz was walking a tightrope. Although the cease-fire was so far at least partially effective, he was feeling pressure from above to restore order and to begin destroying the city. "Our task is hard," Choltitz wrote his wife that night, "and our days grow difficult. I always try to do my duty and must often ask God to help me find the path on which it lies."

In the mind of Hitler, however, the path was clear. His order that day had been adamant: "In history, the loss of Paris always means the loss of France," he declared. "Paris must not fall into the hands of the enemy

except as a field of ruins." "Why should we care if Paris is destroyed," he had asked Jodl. "The Allies, at this very moment, are destroying cities all over Germany with their bombs."

In the meantime, Eisenhower was himself being pressed to alter his strategy. He described his dilemma in a note to the American Army chief of staff, General George C. Marshall, on August 22: "If the enemy tries to hold Paris with any real strength, he would be a constant menace to our flank. If he largely concedes the place, it falls into our hands whether we like it or not." Conscious of the symbolic importance of the French capital, Eisenhower decided to change course, justifying the action in military terms by characterizing it as sending reinforcements to the Resistance fighters inside the city.

He designated the French 2d Armored Division, which was commanded by General Jacques Leclerc and consisted of 2,000 vehicles and 16,000

An American soldier dashes past a knocked-out jeep on the outskirts of Brest, a French port located on the western tip of Brittany. As an important harbor and site of a German U-boat base, Brest was declared by Hitler a fortress city to be held to the death, but the garrison of 38,000 men, led by General Hermann Ramcke, surrendered to the U.S. VIII Corps on September 19, 1944.

soldiers, to lead the way into Paris. With the U.S. 4th Infantry Division moving on the right of the French, the objective was to enter Paris as soon as possible after noon on August 23, at which time the fragile truce between opposing forces in the city was scheduled to end.

The liberating forces met unexpectedly stiff opposition south and west of the capital. Leclerc ordered a small advance force of tanks and half-tracks to be detached to make faster progress. Guided by civilians who removed trees and repaired roads they had torn up to hamper the Germans, the detachment crossed the Seine and entered Paris that night.

On the outskirts of the city, the German defenders faded away when confronted with the Allies, but in Paris itself, Choltitz and his men did not capitulate at first. Several sharp engagements took place, and 2,600 Germans remained at large in the Bois de Boulogne, a forested area six miles west of the heart of the city. The formal end came, finally, about noon on August 25, when French tanks surrounded Choltitz's headquarters at the Hôtel Meurice. The general calmly allowed himself to be taken prisoner. The French whisked him through jeering crowds to the Prefecture of Police, where he signed surrender papers.

The German strongholds across the city gave up one by one. Among the last to surrender were the troops in the Bois de Boulogne, who walked out with their hands up shortly after the triumphal parade on August 26 led by Generals de Gaulle and Leclerc. Three days later, the U.S. 28th Division marched through the city in a show of strength designed to reinforce de Gaulle's claim to leadership of the provisional French government. In any Hollywood movie of the era, the war would have ended on that splendid note. Instead, the troops who passed in review before Bradley and de Gaulle kept on marching and were engaged in battle by the end of the day. The war was far from over.

As August became September, American forces driving up from the south made a long northward thrust just west of the Swiss border. In early September, George Patton's hard-charging Third Army had spearheads across the Meuse River and was aiming for Metz.

With Allied power poised at the frontiers of Germany itself, the time for retreat had ended. The remnants of German Army Groups B and G wheeled to form a northwest-to-southeast defensive line passing through Alsace-Lorraine—along essentially the same line that had been the rear border of OB West on D-day. In the intervening weeks, the Germans had lost some 300,000 soldiers on the western front and nearly 2,200 of the 2,300 tanks and assault guns that had been in service on June 6. Faced with rapidly dwindling resources, Hitler could look only to the Ruhr industrial region for succor. And the Ruhr was the Allies' next objective. ✚

A Nazi General's Plan to Save Paris

In August of 1944, the fate of Paris rested tenuously in the hands of a tough field soldier, General Dietrich von Choltitz. The forty-nine-year-old officer had been handpicked as military commander of Greater Paris by the Führer himself because of his reputation for unswerving loyalty and obedience, built up over twenty-nine years of military service. Choltitz moved into his headquarters in the elegant Hôtel Meurice on Rue de Rivoli on August 9 and began carrying out his mandate to "hold and control the city as a communications hub."

But as the Allied armies surged closer to Paris, Hitler became determined that his last great prize of the war should not be captured intact. He sent in a team of demolition experts to begin blowing up the city's forty-five bridges, as well as its major factories, public utilities, and government buildings, including such landmarks as the Palais du Luxembourg, the Chamber of Deputies, and the Quai d'Orsay.

For the first time, Choltitz wavered in the execution of an order. With the Americans about to cross the Seine north and south of the city, Paris had lost its military value, and he could not destroy it. "What kind of barbarity was I being ordered to do?" he later wrote. "How could a civilized person put such measures into effect?"

So the general who had been ordered to destroy Paris resolved to do everything in his power to save it. He evaded OKW's urgent inquiries about the progress of the demolition, and when the Paris police launched an insurrection on August 19, he negotiated a truce with them. Three days later, street fighting again threatened to boil out of control, and Choltitz sent a secret message to the Allies warning that if they did not come quickly, Paris was doomed. By this time, General Dwight D. Eisenhower had made up his mind to liberate the city.

General Choltitz (*below*) had fought with distinction on both fronts. He led a battalion in the Netherlands, a regiment in the Crimea, a division in the Ukraine, and a corps in Normandy.

Partially shielded by baggage carts, rebellious French policemen, one still in uniform, fire across the Pont Neuf at Germans on the Île de la Cité during the August 19 revolt.

The Arrival of the Liberators

At 9:22 p.m. on August 24, 1944, a small detachment of French armor rolled through Porte d'Italie and proceeded unopposed to the Hôtel de Ville, the Paris city hall. There, members of the Resistance broadcast the electrifying news over the radio: Liberation was at hand. Within minutes the bells of nearby Notre Dame Cathedral, which had been silent for four years, were ringing in wild jubilation. Soon, church bells all across the city of Paris joined in.

The next morning, the U.S. 4th Infantry and the French 2d Armored divisions arrived, crossing the Seine on bridges that General Choltitz had refused to destroy. As the Allied columns passed through the throngs of cheering Parisians, they came within range of the Germans, who were barricaded behind some three dozen of the city's most treasured buildings.

One of the first strongholds to be attacked was the sixty-four-acre Palais du Luxembourg, defended by 700 SS troops and a number of panzers that were dug into the palace gardens. In the meantime, other Allied units surrounded the Chamber of Deputies, the Quai d'Orsay, the École Militaire, the Hôtels Majestic and Crillon, and the areas around the Arc de Triomphe and the Place de la République.

A German Panther tank knocked out of action by a French gunner burns in the Place de la Concorde.

Seemingly heedless of flying
bullets, spectators watch a
French tank fire on the Hôtel
Crillon. The only serious damage
sustained by the building was
the loss of one of the massive
columns along its facade.

German medics wearing Red Cross armbands tend to a wounded comrade in the courtyard of the French Senate inside the Palais du Luxembourg.

Firing celebratory shots into the air, French Resistance fighters herd a group of German prisoners through the Place de l'Opéra. Fearful of being massacred by vengeful citizens, many Germans held out until they could surrender to regular French or American troops.

Seeking an Honorable Surrender

As the Allies went about rooting the Germans out of their strongholds in the city, Colonel Pierre Bilotte of the French 2d Armored Division sent General Choltitz a note, demanding that he "end all resistance" or face "total extermination." Choltitz refused. "I do not accept ultimatums," he replied.

Around noon on August 25, the German commander watched a force composed of 200 French soldiers and five Sherman tanks approach his headquarters in the Hôtel Meurice. "Gentlemen," he told his staff, "our last combat has begun. May God protect you all. I hope the survivors may fall into the hands of regular troops and not those of the population."

After a brief, bitter fight, the French overwhelmed the small garrison. Choltitz, freshly shaven and wearing his dress uniform, awaited them in his office, his soldier's honor intact. As his captors marched him into the street, the crowd shouted obscenities and spat at him. They could not know that the general—a symbol of four years of Nazi oppression—had saved their beautiful city by defying Hitler's vengeful orders to blow it up.

Gathered in anticipation of welcoming their liberators, Parisians scatter for any available cover as snipers open fire from the

buildings surrounding the Place de la Concorde.

The Fate of a Proud Soldier

Choltitz's captors drove him to the Prefecture of Police where he accepted the terms of capitulation prepared by General Jacques Leclerc. Now that he was a prisoner himself, Choltitz could, in honor, agree to Leclerc's proposal that teams of French, German, and American officers go around to the remaining centers of resistance and order the Germans to surrender.

Riding in a loudspeaker van, one multinational team arrived just in time to prevent a bloody assault on the Prince Eugène Barracks, where the harshest fighting of the day had occurred between 1,200 Germans and the French Resistance, assisted by elements of the French 2d Ar-

mored Division. Shortly after six o'clock in the evening, the Germans who were holed up inside of the last stronghold, the French Senate building, ceased firing—although random shooting continued into the night. By then, Choltitz had been whisked away in an American truck to an Allied prison camp.

Three days later, General Walther Model, commander in chief West, asked a Reich tribunal to inaugurate criminal proceedings against Choltitz. He was charged with treason and scheduled to be tried *in absentia*. His officer friends in Germany managed to delay the trial, however, and the war ended before it could convene.

Choltitz leaves the Prefecture of Police with Leclerc in a French half-track after agreeing to the surrender terms. He was taken to 2d Armored Division head-quarters at the Montparnasse station where he signed additional cease-fire orders (*inset*).

 Rettet euch in den
Reichsluftschutzbund
Landesgruppe Groß-Berlin e.V.

ENTWURF: H. LEIBELING   DRUCK u. HOLLERBAUM u. SCHMIDT INH. FRITZ v. LINDENAU BERLIN N 65.

Air War over the Fatherland

The citizens of Hamburg were enjoying a balmy summer evening when the first alarm sounded at 9:20 p.m. on July 24, 1943. When the all clear sounded ten minutes later, many of the city's million and a half residents concluded that their luck was holding: They had experienced more false alarms than serious raids, and no Allied bombers had been over the city since a nuisance raid three weeks earlier.

Business was brisk at the drinking halls and restaurants, and empty tables were scarce at the cafés lining the city's numerous waterways. During the day, strollers had filled the beautiful public parks and gardens, and the world-famous Hagenbeck Zoo. The cinemas were also packed, including the cavernous 3,000-seat Ufa-Palast, Germany's largest. When another alarm sounded at 12:33 a.m., many people were reluctant to head for their shelters, standing instead at windows or doorways to watch. They knew that nighttime aerial bombardments made a spectacular show—as long as the bombs fell on somebody else's neighborhood.

In the early morning of July 25, however, the bombs would fall on many neighborhoods, as 728 British heavy bombers introduced Hamburg to the horrors of a massive air attack. Their target was a logical one: Germany's second-largest city was a center of trade and industry, with aircraft factories, engineering works, and oil refineries. Most important, Hamburg was home to shipyards that had built the heavy cruiser *Admiral Hipper*, the battleship *Bismarck*, and one third of Germany's U-boats.

Those watching the sky saw the first signs of action when British target markers burst open, releasing a cascade of yellow pyrotechnic candles that were visible for miles as they drifted to the ground. The markers were accompanied by illumination flares, whose harsh white glare lit the streets. Searchlights probed the sky for the initial wave of bombers, and flak batteries began hurling shells toward the invisible aircraft.

Within minutes, the first bombs began to fall—high explosives and a rain of incendiaries. Those who had remained to watch the fireworks now rushed to their basements or ran down the streets to public shelters, many carrying suitcases packed with valuables. One couple carefully stayed in

In Hamburg's medieval quarter, Saint Nicholas Church lies in ruins—a victim of the Allied bombs in July 1943. In Hamburg alone, Allied raids destroyed seventeen historic churches.

the shadows. Awed by the unnatural brilliance of the flares and the roar of engines, they seemed afraid that the British bombardiers three miles up in the sky might actually see them and aim a bomb directly at them.

The crowded shelters shook from the blasts. In the streets above, fire-fighters worked against a multitude of small blazes started by incendiaries. Block wardens and motorized teams of Hitler Youth tried to help, but they suffered casualties from high explosives and found the streets blocked by rubble. Soon, hundreds of apartment buildings, stores, and offices—the equivalent of more than fifty miles of street frontage—were ablaze.

When the all clear sounded again at 3:02 a.m., about 1,500 Hamburg residents were dead, and many more were injured. The survivors emerged from their shelters to a scene of utter destruction. Tens of thousands of them were now homeless, and many of the city's landmarks lay in ruins. The Ufa-Palast had burned to the ground. The central police station and long-distance telephone exchange were demolished. Bombs that struck the Hagenbeck Zoo had freed many of the monkeys and left scores of other animals dead, or so badly injured that they had to be destroyed.

The July 25 raid was but the first of ten straight days of around-the-clock bombing directed against the city by the British and Americans. When the bombs finally stopped falling on August 3, about 44,000 civilians were dead, nearly two-thirds of them women and children. More than half of the city's housing units had been destroyed in a massive firestorm, making 900,000 people homeless. Although the U-boat yards received little damage, the breakdown of Hamburg's infrastructure slowed war production. It would take five months for industrial output to return to 80 percent of its preraid levels. The slowdown meant that the German navy would have at least twenty fewer submarines to throw into the Battle of the Atlantic. The Allies called the unrelenting air attack against Hamburg Operation Gomorrah; the Germans knew it simply as the *Katastrophe*, the catastrophe.

The raids that demolished Hamburg were part of an air war that ebbed and flowed across Europe for five years, as Britain, joined later by the United States, mounted a massive campaign to destroy the Reich's industrial centers and crush the morale of its citizens. The effort began in earnest in May 1940, following Hitler's invasion of Belgium, France, and the Netherlands, and came partly in response to a German raid against Rotterdam that killed more than 800 people and destroyed the heart of the city. The following day, May 15, 1940, Winston Churchill, Britain's new prime minister, gave the Royal Air Force (RAF) permission to retaliate, and that night, ninety-nine aircraft of the RAF Bomber Command attacked oil refineries and railroads in the Ruhr Valley.

Because German fighters had taken a heavy toll of British planes during earlier daylight raids against naval targets (they had shot down 20 percent of the attacking aircraft, on average), the RAF now sent its bombers over Germany only at night. As winter approached and the nights grew longer, the British took advantage of the covering darkness to thrust deep into the German heartland. These early raids usually included 100 to 150 aircraft, each instructed to bomb a particular factory or military installation. Routes to the targets, bombing time, and altitude were all to be determined by the individual bomber crews.

Not until late 1941 did the British discover that their methods were producing little success. A photographic survey showed that of the crews that claimed to have bombed their targets, only one in five had hit within five miles of the aiming point, the spot where a bombardier began releasing the bombs. In the smoky, heavily defended Ruhr, the figure was worse—one in ten. In November 1941, Bomber Command ordered a pause in long-range operations.

Stiffening German defenses contributed to the decision. Plans for defending the Reich against air attack had begun in 1935 and were now bearing fruit. The Nazi party apparatus took over responsibility for civil defense, producing plans for air-raid alarms and first-aid services, as well as research on shelter construction. Many believed such measures were unnecessary; Luftwaffe chief Hermann Göring boasted early in the war that if Allied bombers could penetrate his defenses, "then my name is Hermann Meier"—a Jewish name.

Civil defense efforts expanded greatly in September 1940, after a British raid on Berlin in retaliation for German attacks on London. Hitler issued an emergency decree listing eighty-two cities where public shelters and other facilities were to be built. He intended the shelters to augment the basements beneath private homes and apartment blocks that protected about half of the population. For those Germans with no basements, or who happened to be away from home during an attack, there would be special, concrete towers and large, multistory bunkers, built aboveground or dug beneath large commercial or office buildings. Most of these shelters had backup electrical systems to provide lighting and ventilation in case municipal power failed. Civilians also found refuge in the lower floors of the fortresslike flak towers that raised antiaircraft guns above surrounding buildings to give them a clear field of fire.

The core of every city's civil defense organization was its fire and police departments, reinforced by army reservists, usually men who were too old for active military service. Large numbers of auxiliaries, including many Hitler Youth, served with the professionals. Manufacturing companies

Newly decorated antiaircraft auxiliaries, including two wounded youths, attend a funeral for comrades killed in an Allied air raid. By the middle of 1943, as many as 100,000 German youngsters—some of them barely eleven years old—had volunteered to serve in the flak units.

127

were obliged to release workers to help operate the mobile water pumps. Nazi party organizations often provided additional firefighting equipment. Each city block had a warden, who supervised the neighborhood residents in fighting fires with the sand and water that were stored on every floor of the apartment buildings.

The Luftwaffe also recruited civilians, mostly women and teenage boys, to help operate the searchlights and antiaircraft guns. At the beginning of the war, the flak batteries were arranged in a great belt that covered the approaches to Germany from Britain, but when the air raids intensified, the Germans transplanted most of the units to the cities and military installations that the Allies were most likely to target.

The flak batteries met limited success. On average, they had to fire more than 3,300 shells to bring down a single enemy bomber, and many of the weapons could not shoot high enough to reach the highest-flying intruders. Nevertheless, respect for flak concentrations forced Allied pilots to make detours and fly at higher altitudes, with a resulting loss in bombing accuracy. In addition, there was no better morale booster for beleaguered civilians huddled in a shelter than to hear a nearby flak battery hurling shells at their airborne tormenters.

The backbone of the defense against Allied bombers, however, consisted of the aircraft controlled by Luftwaffe Major General Josef Kammhuber, commander of Germany's night air defenses. A technical expert and brilliant organizer, Kammhuber devised an air-defense system that divided the sky over western Germany, Holland, and Belgium into a series of adjacent boxes, called *Räume*. Each box, or *Raum*, was patrolled by a single fighter, usually a twin-engine Junkers 88 or Messerschmitt 110, under the control of a ground radar station.

In turn, each ground radar station was equipped with three radar sets: one long-range, multidirectional Freya radar, with a range-finding device that detected incoming bombers 100 miles away, and two narrow-beam Würzburg radars that could focus on individual aircraft at a distance of 30 miles. One Würzburg tracked the fighter, the other tracked a single enemy bomber; a control officer, monitoring the positions of both aircraft, broadcast directions to the fighter pilot to bring him within two miles of the bomber. From there, the pilot could either make visual contact or use the on-board Lichtenstein radar to close within striking distance. The entire system was called Himmelbett, or four-poster bed, for the four radar devices that were crucial to its success.

Himmelbett was highly effective against the loose aggregations of bombers that typified British raids through 1941. The RAF policy of staggering attacks meant that the German night-fighters could pick off the bombers

one at a time. But when Bomber Command resumed its raids in early 1942, it had a new chief, Sir Arthur Harris, and a new tactic, called Area Bombing. Air Chief Marshal Harris was a leading proponent of the unrestricted bombing of cities. He decreed that targets were no longer to be specific facilities but whole sections of cities, so that every bomb that fell would cause damage—dislocating transportation systems, cutting off telephones, power, and water, and destroying workers' housing.

Harris pursued the Area Bombing program so doggedly that he became known to the public as "Bomber" Harris. His flight crews, who respected him but also were aware of his willingness to absorb casualties, called him "Butch"—short for Butcher.

Instead of aiming at individual targets, every attacking plane now unloaded its bombs on a general aiming point, marked at the beginning of the raid by special Pathfinder aircraft. And instead of approaching the target from various directions at different times, the hundreds of raiders flew to and from their assigned sites in carefully aligned streams, sometimes up to seventy miles long.

The new approach swamped Himmelbett. The concentrated British bomber stream generally passed through only one or two of Kammhuber's boxes. While one night-fighter was overwhelmed by far more planes than it could possibly attack, the night-fighter in the adjacent box saw nothing. Although his 400 night-fighters were still claiming victims (during the first year of Area Bombing, only 30 percent of Harris's crews survived to the end of their twenty-five-mission tour), Kammhuber realized that the growing Allied bomber fleets would overwhelm his defenses.

German defensive problems became more acute in August 1942, with the entrance into the air war of the U.S. Eighth Air Force. Based in Britain, the Americans favored daylight raids. They thought that the British nighttime area raids were too risky for the pilots and the haphazard results too harsh on civilians. By December, the Americans had flown more than 1,500 daytime sorties against targets in occupied France and the Low Countries, placing an additional burden on the Luftwaffe's already strained resources. The Americans began daylight operations over Germany in January 1943 with a sixty-four-plane attack on Wilhelmshaven, the U-boat command base on the North Sea.

The principal American bombers were heavily armed, sturdily built Boeing B-17s, each carrying ten heavy .50-caliber machine guns. Massed in formations of up to fifty-four aircraft, these so-called Flying Fortresses, could chum the sky with a withering defensive fire. In the Wilhelmshaven raid, most of the B-17s hit the target area, and added insult to injury by downing seven German fighters while losing only one plane of their own.

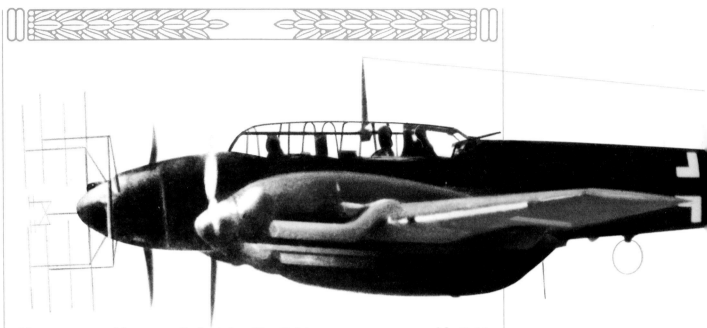

The B-17s would eventually be joined by lighter, more maneuverable B-24 bombers, operating from bases in North Africa and Great Britain.

The Luftwaffe was now fighting around-the-clock, battling the American bombers by day and the British bombers by night. To relieve the pressure on the day-fighters, Göring withdrew 200 fighter planes from the Russian and Mediterranean fronts, increasing the number of aircraft available to defend the Fatherland to approximately 800.

The Germans also developed new daytime tactics. Pilots began to work in teams, with as many as fifty attacking a single bomber formation. After discovering that the B-17 was lightly armed in front, bold Luftwaffe pilots began flying at the Fortresses head-on, allowing the American planes to fill their gunsights before squeezing off a deadly burst of cannon fire. To enable the fighters to make two or more sorties against one attacking force, the Luftwaffe set up auxiliary airfields where they could refuel, rearm, and quickly return to action.

On April 26, 1943, when 107 B-17s attacked a Focke Wulf aircraft factory at Vergesck, near Bremen, the Germans were ready for them. Controllers held back the fighters until they were certain of the Americans' target. As the Flying Fortresses lined up over Vergesck, two Jagdgeschwader, or fighter groups, slashed through the formation from dead ahead, ignoring their own flak, then circled around to repeat the attack. The German fighters continued their ferocious onslaught even as the bombers staggered over the North Sea on their way home. By the end of the day, they and the flak batteries had destroyed 16 American aircraft and damaged 48 more. The Germans lost only 5 fighters.

Faced with mounting losses, American commanders began to focus their bombing campaign on the Luftwaffe itself, moving aircraft factories, plane storage areas, and the essential ball-bearing industry to the top of their target lists. Most of these facilities, however, were located in central and southern Germany and required a long flight over hostile territory. The attacks that began in August 1943 produced some damage, but the German fighters chopped up the American formations. They shot down 60 bombers over Schweinfurt and Regensburg on August 17, and 30 more that attacked

Lichtenstein radar devices, like the one added to the nose of this Messerschmitt 110 *(opposite)*, enabled German fighters to home in on enemy bombers. Converted to a night-fighter in 1941 as part of the Himmelbett system, each Me 110 prowled a twenty-mile zone of air space. Meanwhile, Würzburg radar dishes *(right)* relayed the positions of the fighter, and the bomber it was pursuing, to anti-aircraft division headquarters. There, both planes' paths were plotted on a glass-topped table *(below)* by color-coded beams of light—red for an enemy bomber, blue for a German fighter.

A Messerschmitt 110 (*top right*) swoops across the sky in hot pursuit of an Allied daylight bomber (*left*) in this remarkable

photograph taken from the cockpit of an American B-17.

the railroad center at Münster on October 11. Three days later, 291 Flying Fortresses again struck Schweinfurt; 60 failed to return. Some 300 German fighters hounded the American force to and from the target, leaving a trail of shattered B-17s across Belgium, Luxembourg, Germany, and France; among those bombers that made it back, 17 were damaged beyond repair, and another 121 had suffered lesser damage. No air force could long survive such casualties, and the Americans halted the raids deep inside Germany.

The reprieve for the Luftwaffe's day-fighters was brief. The seeds of an American resurgence had been sown as early as July 30, 1943, during a raid on the Focke Wulf aircraft engine and assembly plants at Kassel. As German fighters harassed the withdrawing Eighth Air Force bombers, they were met over the German-Dutch border by more than 100 American P-47 Thunderbolts whose range had been extended by extra fuel tanks. Surprised in the act of picking off damaged bombers, the Germans lost 9 planes while shooting down only 1 Thunderbolt. From that time on, P-47s began escorting bomber formations to and from the German border, and by early 1944, a new American fighter had extended the protection across the length and breadth of the Reich. The single-engine P-51 Mustang was sturdy, fast, and maneuverable, a match for the best German fighters, with endurance that could take it to virtually any target in Germany.

In the meantime, the Luftwaffe still had to contend with the British night-bombers. Back in June 1943, night-fighter chief Kammhuber had proposed beefing up the Himmelbett defense networks by tripling the number of night-fighters in addition to adding new radar and control systems—projects that would challenge Germany's already strained aircraft and electronics manufacturers. Luftwaffe chief Göring, who had long believed the exacting Kammhuber expected too large a share of the Reich's scarce manpower and aircraft, transferred him to a backwater post in Norway.

Major Hajo Herrmann, the Luftwaffe pilot who developed the Wild Boar tactics—the idea of lone night-fighters roving above target cities to intercept Allied bombers—was notorious for his bold thinking. He once proposed attacking the United States with seaplanes that would take on fuel and bombs from U-boats stationed off the East Coast.

Kammhuber's subordinates, however, had already begun to test new tactics that would allow the night-fighters to pursue targets without assistance from radar. Such methods became crucial in mid-1943, when the British bombers began blinding German radar by dumping into the sky large quantities of aluminum-coated paper that fed a myriad of false echoes into Himmelbett. The British called their new system Window. The Germans dubbed it Düppel, after the town where they identified it. Used for the first time in the Hamburg raids of July and August, Window baffled the

Me 109s line up on the runway in preparation for a Wild Boar mission. Night operations required these single-seat day-fighters to carry extra fuel tanks in order to extend their normal 620-mile range.

German night-fighter controllers and flak batteries, cutting British bomber losses by 30 percent.

The British advantage was short lived, however. Anxious to prevent another Hamburg, Göring decided to try an idea proposed by a relatively junior pilot, Major Hans-Joachim (Hajo) Herrmann. Herrmann wanted to oppose the Bomber Command raiders with single-seat day-fighters flown by bomber pilots, experienced in night flying. Instead of using radar and ground control to intercept raiders on their way to and from the target, Herrmann's fighters would operate directly over the city while the attack was in progress. Climbing high above the bomber stream, the pilots would watch for bombers silhouetted against the brilliant glare of the city below, eerily lit up by a combination of searchlight beams, marker flares, and burning buildings. Because their success depended on their own roving efforts, these fighters came to be called *Wilde Sau*, or Wild Boars.

Herrmann, flying a Focke Wulf 190, led a Wild Boar mission over the Ruhr Valley on July 30, 1943. Before taking off, he had arranged to have the flak gunners in the region restrict their fire to below 20,000 feet. But the pursuit of the British bombers carried the German fighters over the city of Cologne, where no such agreement existed. In the air space below him, Herrmann saw a number of bombers pinned in the merciless beams of searchlights, with flak exploding all around them. But heavy antiaircraft fire was nothing new to Herrmann and his former bomber pilots. Without hesitation, they flew into the thick of the friendly fire. Closing behind a brightly lit Lancaster, Herrmann was buffeted by flak bursts and nearly blinded by the searchlights. "It was like sitting in a cage of fire and glowing steel," he later reported. The attention of the bomber's rear gunner was focused on the burning city below; in his experience, there was no need for vigilance: The German fighters never attacked over the target. A burst of shells from

135

Herrmann's four cannon interrupted the gunner's reverie, and sent the Lancaster plunging to the ground in flames.

Herrmann's successful attack was just one of many, and soon, whole squadrons of day-fighters were flying after dark, using his Wild Boar tactics. Because the single-seat FW 190s lacked the fuel capacity to remain aloft patrolling for enemy aircraft, the pilots worked a variation on the theme, called *Zahme Sau*, or Tame Boar. This tactic required the fighters to seek out their prey with guidance from ground controllers, who could still discern the general location of the bomber stream—although Window prevented the tracking of individual aircraft. Once fighter pilots had located the general position of the attackers by radio beacons, they could find their targets either visually or with airborne radar. If they lost contact, they could tune in on the running directions provided by the ground controllers and relocate the bomber stream.

The ground controllers were only part of the fighter pilots' support network, which began functioning long before any enemy bombers were in the air. The Luftwaffe knew that Bomber Command could not strike deep into Germany on short summer nights, and they also knew that major bombing raids seldom came during a full moon. By studying the weather and patterns of recent raids, analysts could get a fair idea of when and where an Allied raid might occur.

The first sign of a pending attack came during the day, when electronic monitoring stations picked up signals from radio and radar equipment on RAF bombers being checked out at British airfields. If the volume of traffic was heavy, night-fighter units were warned in the early evening to be ready for another raid. When the British crews boarded their planes and began to warm up their electronic gear, the Germans knew that takeoff was imminent. The monitoring stations then tracked the pulses from the bombers' radar sets, establishing the approximate path of the bomber stream even before it was picked up by the German coastal radar stations. Fighter controllers received and passed on a constant flow of such information, as well as radar reports and visual sightings by reconnaissance planes.

By the autumn of 1943, German fighter pilots using the new tactics once again dominated the night skies over the Reich. During three major raids on Berlin in August and September, they brought down 123 bombers and damaged another 114, representing 14 percent of the aircraft committed. It was a loss rate the British could not sustain for long.

The reign of the Wild Boar was short, however. Winter brought bad weather and poor visibility, conditions day-fighters were ill equipped to handle. Pilots frequently got lost and sometimes had to bale out when their planes ran out of fuel before they could find an airfield. Those who found

"We greet the first worker of Germany: Adolf Hitler," reads a banner strung across a ruined building in Berlin for Hitler's fifty-fifth birthday on April 20, 1944. The Führer himself never bothered to visit a single bombed-out city in the Reich.

en den erften Arbeiter Deutfchlands: Adolf hitler!

a place to land still had to contend with clouds and fog and often crashed during their approach.

By the spring of 1944, both the night- and the day-fighter wings were in a sorry state. During the months of February and March, the Luftwaffe suffered 945 fighter-pilot casualties, with the day-fighters alone losing 444 killed or missing, along with 244 wounded—50 percent of their total effective strength. Replacing the planes was not a problem; in fact, aircraft production had increased rapidly in 1944 as the industry dispersed its factories to minimize air-raid damage. Replacing the veteran pilots was another matter. The Luftwaffe threw new men into the fray without adequate training, and the losses mounted further.

Even more devastating to the German air operations was the aviation fuel shortage that resulted from persistent Allied bombing of the Reich's oil and gasoline facilities. Entire fighter groups were grounded for lack of fuel.

By May 1944, the Americans were sending off as many as 1,000 P-51 fighters at a time on missions over Germany, while the Luftwaffe could put fewer than 300 fighters of all types into the air. So great was the American advantage that the Mustangs turned from defensive escort duty to offensive operations. Effective German fighter resistance had ended.

The Luftwaffe's dwindling defenses exposed German cities to around-the-clock pounding. The port city of Kiel suffered extensive damage, and repeated attacks on Frankfurt am Main destroyed the center of that city, as well as large parts of the surrounding area. Nor were smaller cities exempt. In Friedrichshafen, a town of 28,000 that was the site of several aircraft and tank factories, American bombers left behind twenty cubic yards of rubble for every resident.

The very regularity of the Allied raids made them an ordinary part of urban life. Radio broadcasts reported the course of bomber formations, and no conversation was complete without speculation on the likelihood and timing of that night's raid. Most citizens preferred an attack that ended early, allowing time for a peaceful supper and sleep.

A woman visitor to the German capital in 1944 discovered that the Berliners found some measure of comfort in the precision of the American daylight bombers. While riding on an elevated train, she wondered why the passing platforms were becoming increasingly deserted, until a man who was seated across from her looked up from his paper, glanced at his watch and then the sky, and remarked that a raid seemed imminent: "Twelve o'clock, punctual as usual."

As the visitor hurried from the train at the next stop, the howl of sirens and the hum of 1,000 approaching bombers filled the air. The hum soon became a remorseless roar. She followed signs to a public shelter, which turned out to be a narrow, concrete-lined trench covered with a tin roof. A bomb explosion hurled her through the entrance onto the lap of an elderly woman, who was methodically counting to herself as the shelter rocked like a boat in a storm. When the count reached eight, the old lady relaxed. Each plane's bomb bay held just eight bombs, she confided. There would be peace until the next wave of bombers arrived.

In the aftermath of the worst raids, some citizens criticized the Nazi regime that had brought them to such a pass, but the mood of the population usually improved with the arrival of relief trains and trucks bringing kettles of soup and sandwiches made with scarce butter and sausage. City workers could usually restore water, gas, electricity, and train service within a few days. Residents who had fled to the suburbs and nearby countryside filtered back into town to resume their daily routines. Those who had lost homes and possessions simply moved into the shelters, going to work by day. One Cologne bunker was even the site of a wedding; after the ceremony, the bride and groom mounted a bicycle to ride to their crosstown honeymoon refuge.

Many city dwellers, however, had long since departed. The evacuation of women and children from the worst-hit cities had begun in 1942, when more than one million moved to camps and homes in rural Germany. The most fortunate found shelter with relatives and friends; whatever the difficulties of leaving home, they were at least sure of comfortable lodging, food, and quiet nights. Others were less fortunate. Lodging with strangers

Bound for the relative safety of rural education camps, two youngsters bid reluctant good-byes to their fathers before boarding a train leaving Berlin in July 1943. They were among the 2.5 million children who were evacuated from German cities during the war.

far from their homes, they had to contend with cramped quarters, skimpy meals, and quaint local customs. Irritations arose between the refugees and their hosts, with many rural folk angered at having their lives disrupted. Despite the friction, many refugees settled in, helping with chores and making friends while trying to stay in touch with loved ones left behind.

In the crumbling cities, shortages grew worse than those found in the countryside, where fresh food was easier to come by. In early 1943, Minister of Propaganda Joseph Goebbels announced in a ringing speech that the Reich was now engaged in *Totaler Krieg*, or total war. Henceforth, all efforts were to be directed toward military production. To release employees for war work, many industries and nonessential businesses curtailed their hours of operation or shut down completely. New laws set limits on the manufacture of nonmilitary items, and some luxury goods—including jewelry and musical instruments—were banned outright. By the end of the year, the demands of the military had left little coal for domestic heating and made new clothes and shoes almost impossible to find. To reduce the demand on the bomb-ravaged electrical system, authorities decreed that burned-out light bulbs could only be exchanged for new ones of less wattage. It was a moot point; light bulbs and electrical fuses were already so hard to find that workers stole them from their offices, ignoring official threats of prosecution.

Despite periodic reductions in food rations, most people ate enough to keep going. The food was far inferior in quality and quantity to what Germans had been able to purchase early in the war. White bread was now a luxury, separately rationed; in most loaves, wheat was mixed with barley or rye. Margarine replaced the butter ration in early 1943, and later that year, the egg quota fell to one per month. In the same period, lemons and oranges disappeared from grocery shelves, their availability cut off by the surrender of Italy. Even potatoes, a staple of the German diet, became scarce after bad weather ruined the 1943 harvest. Factory kitchens, relying on stews to feed their workers, were particularly hard hit, and the government immediately began to ferret out hoarded potato supplies.

Germans grew more fatalistic as the war progressed. By 1944, most city dwellers had survived at least one horrendous raid, and that common experience produced a solidarity that exceeded the Nazis' wildest hopes. The spirit, however, grew less from patriotic fervor than from the weary conviction that no matter what happened, life must go on. The antipathy toward the Allied bombers was leavened with bitterness toward the regime, often expressed in popular songs and doggerel. One ditty that recounted the trials of daily life in a bombed city, and the nightly terror of air raids, ended with this verse: "Feeling gloomy, dearest friends? / Why, our victory

Martyrs of the White Rose

An undercurrent of dissatisfaction with the Nazi regime rippled through the student body at the University of Munich in the spring of 1942. Medical student Hans Scholl, twenty-five, had already begun to bridle at Hitler's demand for "blind obedience and absolute discipline" when he read copies of the bishop of Münster's sermons condemning the Nazi extermination of incurably ill mental patients.

"Finally, a man has had the courage to speak out," Scholl exclaimed. He was determined to add his own voice to the cause. With the support of his friend

Christoph Probst and several others, Scholl began printing and distributing antigovernment leaflets.

Scholl's younger sister Sophie had been at the university for only six weeks when someone handed her a pamphlet entitled *Letters of the White Rose*. "Offer passive resistance," the text urged, "to stop the spread of this atheistic war machine." When Sophie discovered that her brother was the author, she joined him. During the following months, the White Rose—a name chosen for its suggestion of purity—distributed thousands of leaflets throughout Germany.

In February 1943, Hans and Sophie dropped

leaflets from atop a lecture hall. A university porter, a local Nazi party member, spotted the blizzard of paper and called the police. Minutes later, the siblings were apprehended and taken to Gestapo headquarters. Probst was arrested later.

After four days of unrelenting interrogation and a brief trial, the three youths were declared guilty of treason on February 22; that afternoon, they were beheaded.

Although the White Rose had not, as hoped, stirred the German people to action, many hearts echoed the sentiment behind the dying words of Hans Scholl: "Long live freedom!"

White Rose members Hans Scholl (*left*), his sister Sophie, and friend Christoph Probst confer in Munich in July 1942.

is sure! / Over the slogan 'Stick it out,' / Just write the headline Total War.''

Goebbels's propaganda machine struggled to put the best face on the suffering. The Nazi party made sure that civilian heroes received medals for their actions. The press was filled with accounts of heroic deeds, but only hinted at the damage that the Allied bombers were inflicting. In April of 1944, Goebbels himself tried to capture the feelings of people enduring privation under the bombs in an article entitled ''Life Goes On.'' He had never been so proud of Berlin, he wrote, as in the aftermath of the raids. With transportation cut off, he saw streams of people walking to work, the men dirty and unshaven after a night of firefighting, the women lugging bags of utensils for their daily needs. The terror bombing, as Goebbels

Propaganda Minister Joseph Goebbels *(in trenchcoat, left)* inspects bomb damage in Berlin. "It is surprising that Goebbels was everywhere cordially greeted in the streets," reported a press aide after accompanying him on a similar sojourn in 1943. "These suffering men and women feel that at least one of the nation's leaders is interested in their fate."

called it, had given Berlin and the other bombed cities of the Reich a chance to show their unity and strength. "If one were to recount all the sorrow that these bombing nights have brought, one could fill whole libraries. But in spite of this, life goes on."

At least Goebbels's optimism was founded on experience. The little propaganda master was the only Nazi leader who regularly visited bombed neighborhoods. Other officials hesitated to do so, often with good reason. When Göring went to Hamburg a few days after the disastrous 1943 raids, he was greeted with cries of "Hermann Meier"—a derisive reference to his earlier boasts about the Luftwaffe's invincible defenses. Perhaps in deference to the suffering that Hamburg citizens had already endured, on this occasion the gibes went unpunished.

As the cities reeled under the Allied onslaught, Luftwaffe leaders struggled to create a weapon that might even the odds again. The result was the Me 262, a jet fighter with far greater speed and climbing ability than the best Allied fighters. The Messerschmitt factory at Augsburg had been working on the sleek twin-engine plane since 1938, but with only sporadic official support; in the early years of the war, Hitler and the Luftwaffe Design and Testing Command were cautious about introducing a radical new aircraft type. The Me 262 passed a series of trials in late 1942, and in the spring of 1943, Luftwaffe Major General Adolf Galland, commander of the Luftwaffe's fighters, flew it for the first time. Galland was hugely impressed by the plane's performance and reported to Göring that it would put the Luftwaffe "way out in front." "The aircraft," he said, "opens up entirely new possibilities as far as tactics are concerned."

Galland suggested curtailing the development of other fighters so that scarce materials and other resources could be concentrated on the manufacture of the new jets. One-fourth of German fighter production, he argued, should be devoted to the Me 262. Hitler, however, refused to gamble on untested technology. And when he established a modest production rate of sixty per month, the overburdened Messerschmitt works could not reach even that quota.

But Galland refused to give up. At his urging, the Führer attended a demonstration of the aircraft in November 1943. Hitler came away enthralled. Almost overnight, he became one of the plane's most ardent proponents, although it soon became clear that he did not share Galland's ideas about the Me 262's role. Never enamored of defensive strategies or weapons, Hitler wanted a fighter-bomber, a vastly more capable version of the ground attack planes that had chewed up enemy forces during the heady days of Blitzkrieg.

The Führer's directive only added to the confusion at the Messerschmitt works. The landing gear would have to be reinforced to handle the added weight of bombs; auxiliary fuel tanks would be needed to provide a useful bombing radius; bomb release clips, bombsights, and the associated electrical wiring would all have to be designed and built. Furthermore, chronic shortages of nickel and chromium required for high-temperature alloys slowed production of the plane's Jumo 004 engines. There were additional problems with the airframe design and a host of smaller bugs that had never been worked out.

The first Me 262s to see combat were part of a test detachment sent aloft to intercept high-altitude British reconnaissance aircraft in April 1944. In August, Me 262s bombed Allied ground forces in France. The following month, the Luftwaffe assigned thirty of the jets to a fighter unit under Major Walther Nowotny, an ace with 250 victories. *Kommando Nowotny* immediately began operations against the Americans from bases in northern Germany. In its first month of operation, Kommando Nowotny made twenty-two kills, an impressive total for a unit whose pilots had little prior experience flying the revolutionary aircraft.

But Allied fighters were quick to discover the Me 262's Achilles heel: The plane was relatively slow during takeoffs and landings. Soon Mustangs began loitering over the Kommando airfields, and on October 7, they drew blood, shooting down three of the jets. Mechanical failures and accidents claimed more planes, and on November 8, four more jets were shot down. Major Nowotny was one of the casualties, crashing in flames after engaging an American bomber formation escorted by Mustangs. The unit was temporarily withdrawn after five weeks of action, twenty-six of its thirty planes lost or grounded. In November, Hitler finally yielded to the Luftwaffe and allowed it to begin producing Me 262s as fighters. He still demanded, however, that each plane be equipped to carry a 550-pound bomb.

The surviving pilots of Kommando Nowotny formed the nucleus of new, stronger units that went into action in early 1945. Some of their planes were armed with a new air-to-air rocket, the R4M. The unguided R4M carried a two-pound warhead that detonated on impact, with an explosion powerful enough to inflict lethal damage on a heavy bomber. A single Me 262 carried twenty-four R4Ms on simple underwing racks; launched in salvos, they formed a dense pattern like a shotgun blast, with a high probability of scoring at least one hit. The pilots developed new combat methods suited to their speedy fighters: Diving at 530 miles per hour through enemy fighter screens, they pulled up below and behind the bombers, then throttled back and climbed to cut their speed so they would not be going too fast for a good shot when they closed in for the kill.

Although the new tactics and armament made the Me 262s lethal hunt-

The world's first jet aircraft to engage in combat, the Me 262 was considered a design and engineering marvel. Although Messerschmitt produced some 1,300 of these planes before the end of the war, they came too late to stop the flood of Allied bombers over Germany.

ers, they were too few in number and arrived too late to make a significant difference in the air war. By early 1945, only about 1,300 had been built—fewer than the total number of Allied bombers participating in a single raid. It was a good day when 30 jets could fly against the Allies, although large numbers were now rolling off the assembly lines in southern Germany. Most planes were grounded by a lack of fuel, which was available but could not be transported over the bomb-damaged rail lines and highways.

One of the last Me 262 units was Jagdgeschwader 44, assembled in late March 1945 under the command of General Galland, the erstwhile fighter chief who had been relieved of command a few months earlier after more disagreements with Göring. Galland's unit had only a single squadron of planes, but his pilots included many of Germany's top surviving aces, most of them former commanders of fighter groups that had been grounded for lack of fuel. Ending the war at the controls of the world's best fighter plane, these brave men wrote the last tragic chapter for the once proud Luftwaffe.

As its defenses crumbled, the Nazi government began to tout new armaments that would stave off defeat, and perhaps even turn the tide of battle. Reflecting Hitler's obsession with attacking the Allies, these weapons would once more carry the war to Britain, whose Area Bombing campaign had destroyed so many German cities. London would be the main target for these so-called Vengeance Weapons, which the world would come to know as the V-1 and V-2.

The V-weapons were a study in contrasts. The V-1 was a small, pilotless jet airplane with a one-ton warhead and a range of about 200 miles. Its design was so simple that only nine months elapsed between the beginning of work on the project and the first flight—on Christmas Eve in 1942. The V-2 resembled the V-1 only in its range and the size of its warhead. It was a ballistic missile, an expensive and complex device powered by a rocket engine and steered by a sophisticated guidance system. Developing the V-2 took more time: Three years of intensive work, including several spectacular crashes, preceded its first successful launch in October 1942. Because neither weapon could be aimed precisely, they would be used only against city-sized targets, where they would cause some damage no matter where they hit.

The V-1 was the first to be placed in operational use. Originally scheduled for action in early 1944, its deployment was delayed by the repeated Allied bombing of its development and launch sites. The first V-1s were hastily fired on June 13, just a week after the Normandy invasion. Engineers estimated it would take the flying bombs twenty-five minutes to reach their aiming point, London's Tower Bridge. But of the V-1s hurled from their catapults that June dawn, four immediately crashed to earth. The others shot off into the darkness, their engines glowing and emitting a pulsating roar; two of these plummeted into the English Channel, but the remaining four stayed on course for London.

Forewarned by intelligence reports of a new German weapon, RAF Fighter Command knew trouble was coming when radar picked up the four V-1s as they crossed the Kentish coast. The few civilians who happened to see or hear a V-1, however, had no idea what it was. They heard an unusual noise, like that of an old jalopy chugging up a hill; looking up, they saw a fiery streak low in the sky. One schoolboy in east London, awakened by an air-raid alarm, thought he was watching a crippled Luftwaffe raider with a blazing tail. That V-1 came down in nearby Bethnal Green, killing three people and knocking down a railroad bridge. The other three crashed and exploded far from London.

This first attack, hurriedly mounted to meet a deadline that had been set by Hitler, showcased all of the V-1's worst traits, from its tendency to crash on takeoff to the unreliable autopilots that kept most of the bombs from landing anywhere near the target. Its sole success was so isolated that for most Londoners the attack might never have happened; none realized that a new secret weapon had been unleashed. They would learn, to their sorrow, three days later.

Late on the night of June 15, the Germans began a massive V-1 attack. By noon the next day, they had launched 244 flying bombs. Nearly one-fourth crashed soon after takeoff, but many more made it to England. In London, the air-raid alert sounded just before midnight; by morning, when the all clear had not sounded, it became evident that something unusual was happening. People going to work got their first glimpses of the small missiles, sputtering flame and producing a peculiar stuttering roar. Sometimes the sound would stop suddenly, as the flying bomb nosed over into

Luftwaffe Major General Adolf Galland, pictured here *(center)* surrounded by his officers, became the strongest advocate of the Me 262. When he test-flew the jet in 1943, he described the experience as "flying on the wings of an angel."

a dive ending in a huge explosion that leveled buildings and cracked windows a quarter-mile away.

By day's end, seventy-three V-1s had landed in London, and they kept on coming at a steady rate. Sleepless due to constant air-raid alerts, Londoners gathered in shelters where they speculated about the new threat, already dubbed "buzz bombs" or "doodlebugs." In the streets above, damage to homes, factories, and public buildings mounted. Thousands were already homeless, and several hundred were dead. On Sunday, June 18, a V-1 slammed into the Guards Chapel at Wellington Barracks, home of the Royal Guards. The blast killed 119 people who had been attending a service and injured 141. Crowds of shaken citizens gathered to watch rescue workers pull the victims from the rubble, located only a short walk from Parliament and Downing Street. The next day, Churchill ordered the immediate evacuation of the House of Commons from its ancient quarters to a more substantial steel structure.

By the end of June, more than 800 V-1s had hit the city of London. Nearly 2,000 people were dead, thousands of homes were destroyed, and the constant air-raid alerts had cut production in London factories. British spirits had been lifted by the Allied landings at Normandy, and many believed victory was close at hand. But the new aerial assaults dampened such thoughts and plunged the nation into an anxious mood reminiscent of that which had prevailed during the Battle of London in 1940 and 1941. As they had during that first battle, civilians fled the city for safer regions.

More than one million people left London during the summer of 1944.

In Germany, the announcement of the V-1 attacks briefly boosted the morale of a population hungry for good news. "At last, our revenge against England has begun," one elated civilian wrote to a soldier at the front. But the British soon meted out their own revenge.

In June, 2,500 RAF bombers unleashed the heaviest raid to date on Berlin.

German soldiers (*below*) roll a V-1 flying bomb out of its hideaway in the French countryside in August 1944. To conceal the V-1s from the eyes of Allied pilots, the launch sites were well camouflaged in orchards and farmyards. Germans built some sixty-four sites along the northwest coast of France. From there, the flying bombs, such as the one about to hit London at right, were a mere twenty-five-minute flight from England.

The next day, the Americans followed suit, sending 1,000 bombers accompanied by 1,200 fighters. By noon, smoke from the burning capital had turned a bright summer sky to twilight. The damage was far greater than the V-1 could ever do to London, and some dispirited civilians began to mutter that V actually stood for *Versager*, or failure.

In addition to striking back, the RAF moved quickly to bolster its defenses against the V-1s, concentrating antiaircraft guns, barrage balloons, and fighter forces southeast of London. The first squadron of British jet fighters joined the melee, knocking out thirteen flying bombs in a month. Later, fighters assigned to chase V-1s were stripped of armor and all excess weight in order to boost their speed. Pilots soon found that shooting down a V-1 was hazardous work, however, because the blast from its powerful warhead could blow them out of the sky. A safer tactic was to pull up alongside the speedy missile, slide a wing under its wing, and then execute a roll, tipping the buzz bomb off course. This violent motion would jar the V-1s sensitive autopilot, throwing the missile into a fatal spin.

The Luftwaffe replied by attempting to overwhelm the British defenses with salvos of V-1s. Although the tactic met with brief success—a total of 101 buzz bombs hit London on August 3—the defenders soon found ways to counter it, and the daily average of hits fell to about 25. Even that number began to shrink in late August, as advancing Allied troops threatened to overrun the Pas-de-Calais launch sites. On August 26, London enjoyed its

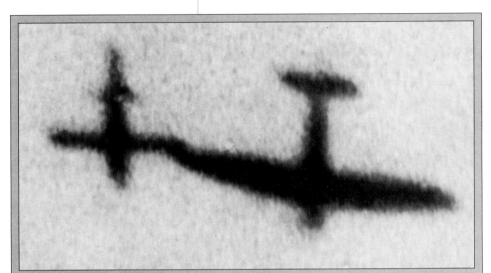

Rocketing over a patchwork of English farmland, a V-1 flying bomb *(opposite, top right)* outstrips an Allied Spitfire XIV. One British pilot, after intercepting a V-1 for the first time, reported, "My first impression was of a white-hot stovepipe. It seemed to get along straight and level as if nothing in heaven or earth would move it from its course." But Allied pilots soon developed a daring technique, captured on film above, of tipping the V-1 off course by positioning the wing of their plane just under the bomb's wing.

first day in eleven weeks without a flying-bomb attack. Only 4 or 5 a day got through before the last catapults were captured on September 1. After withstanding 2,419 V-1 hits, Londoners breathed a collective sigh of relief.

The reprieve lasted only one week. On the evening of September 8, a huge explosion rocked the west London suburb of Chiswick. Residents staggered out of their homes to find a crater thirty feet wide and ten feet deep in the middle of the road, surrounded by ruined houses. There had been no air-raid alert, no telltale buzz-bomb sound—nothing but the blast that killed three people and injured twenty others. Civil defense officials hinted that it might have been a gas-main explosion, but no one believed them. The suspicion quickly spread that the long-heralded V-2 had finally come to London—as it had.

The rocket that hit Chiswick was one of a pair fired from The Hague in the Netherlands just five minutes earlier. During their 200-mile flight to London, the V-2s reached a maximum altitude of 55 miles before slamming to earth at 3,500 miles per hour. They were the first of more than 500 V-2s that would hit London by the end of March 1945. In that seven-month period, scarcely a day passed without the abrupt boom of exploding rockets, sometimes one or two, sometimes five or more. Once again, death and destruction became part of the city's daily life.

The V-2 was a truly terrifying weapon because it literally struck from out of the blue. The rocket traveled faster than sound; therefore, its blast was heard before the noise of its passage through the air, which many likened to the sound of a speeding express train. There was no way to hide from a weapon that could not be seen or heard, nor was there any defense against it. As one wag put it, "If you heard it, the rocket hadn't hit you; if it hit you, you hadn't heard it." Allied attacks against launch sites in the Netherlands proved fruitless, since the V-2's mobile firing platforms required only a flat surface—a road or a forest clearing would do—and could be packed up and driven away within an hour after the missiles were launched. The only V-2 ever shot down was climbing slowly just seconds after its launch when it passed through a formation of American B-24s returning from a raid. A burst of machine-gun fire from one of the bombers sent the projectile tumbling earthward.

The V-2s made the last winter of the war a miserable one for Londoners. Ironically, the rockets actually disrupted life less than the buzz bombs, since there were no air-raid alerts to send the workers to their shelters. But they caused severe hardship in addition to casualties. The sudden booms of exploding rockets made people edgy and angry. No one coined clever nicknames for the V-2.

Goebbels's propaganda machine gloated over every V-weapon success. "The explosions not only smashed whole rows of houses," said a German radio broadcast, "they pulverized everything—tiles, bricks, stones, and especially glass." Such boasts rang hollow, however, in the Reich's anguished cities, whose residents were all too familiar with pulverized buildings. All but the most fervent Nazis realized that no matter what destruction the V-weapons wrought, they would not turn the tide of the war.

As the Russians advanced through eastern Germany in early 1945 and the English and Americans closed in from the west, German cities suffered unrelenting aerial bombardment—three raids a day in some places. The Allies attacked Berlin, harassing it with British Mosquito fighter-bombers between attacks by B-17s, B-24s, and Lancasters. In mid-February, a series of firebomb raids touched off a firestorm that leveled Dresden. The flames killed more than 30,000 civilians, many of them refugees who, ironically, thought they had found a haven.

Civilians attempting to flee the cities found it a risky endeavor; hundreds of Allied fighter planes prowled the skies, firing at almost anything that moved. Few daylight train trips ended without at least one strafing incident, and driving in the countryside became an exercise in watching the sky while speeding past the burned-out hulks of cars and buses.

Most Germans stayed where they were, patiently waiting for the war to end. The smallest corner of home, one Berliner wrote, was better than a palace somewhere else: "If they destroy our living room, we move into the kitchen. If they knock the kitchen apart, we move over into the hallway. If only we can stay at home."

The last massive raid against Berlin came on April 20, Hitler's fifty-sixth birthday. Afterward, the ruined city lay quiet, its electricity, gas, and sewage systems destroyed, its transportation at a virtual halt. Haggard residents waited wearily in long queues to obtain what little food was available; their drinking water came from fire hydrants. Three weeks later, the shooting finally stopped. The words of one Berliner evoked the feelings of all those who emerged from the rubble alive: "We have survived what seemed like the end of the world." ✛

One of Hitler's so-called super-weapons, a V-2—also known as an A4 rocket—hurtles skyward from its test-launch site in Peenemünde, Germany. With a top speed of 3,500 miles per hour, the V-2 was impossible to intercept in flight, but it experienced a high percentage of technical failures. Of 4,000 V-2s fired at London, about 1,000 of them reached southern England.

Life in a "World Gone Mad"

"It was like a medieval picture of hellfire," wrote diarist Ursula von Kardorff of the inferno that engulfed Berlin following an Allied bombing raid. "The fires raged through the night, drowning whatever moans might otherwise have filled the air," recalled Ils Mar Garthaus, a ballerina at the Bremen Opera House, about an attack on her city. Of yet another air assault, Hamburg's police commissioner simply said: "No imagination will ever be able to comprehend the scenes of terror."

But scenes of unimaginable terror became commonplace in Germany as civilians bore the brunt of the most destructive bombing campaign in history. Of the more than one million tons of bombs that the Allies dropped, only 12 percent hit war-related industries. Fully half fell on residential areas, destroying 3.6 million dwellings, killing or seriously injuring more than one million people, and leaving another 7.5 million homeless. These figures are only estimates. The general collapse of German recordkeeping during the final year of war make accurate statistics impossible to come by.

The survivors faced added horrors: charred bodies scattered on the ground, the faint tapping of people trapped beneath the ruins, and as film actress Hildegard Neff gruesomely wrote, the "sweet, fatty smell of the buried, not yet dug out." A Hamburg man was haunted by the memory of rats, grown "fat and fresh" from feeding on corpses, and of swarms of flies. "Their rustling and humming," he recalled, "was the first thing we heard as we awoke."

Life in Germany became a primitive, precarious struggle for existence. City dwellers slept fully clothed so they would not have to waste precious time dressing when the sirens sounded. They learned to hoard food and water and save scraps of wood for cooking fires. And after every raid, they set about cleaning up rubble and unearthing the dead. "Like marionettes on strings, every day the same show: scratching about in the ashes, digging, burying," wrote Garthaus, the Bremen ballerina. "There was no time for complaints," she added. "Only the children gave vent to a plaintive wailing in a world that seemed to have gone completely mad."

"We're alive," writes a young woman on the ruins of her

bombed-out home, hoping that absent relatives may see the message.

Clutching their bundled
belongings, a Munich couple
flees past a burning building.
Their city, the cradle of Hitler's
National Socialist movement,
endured nine major air attacks.

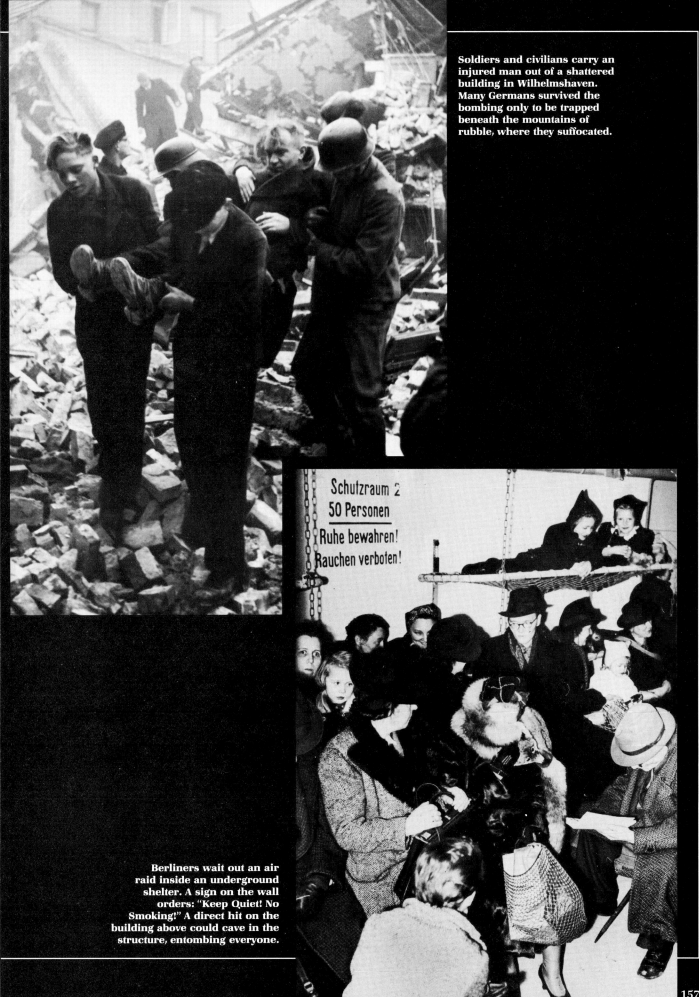

Soldiers and civilians carry an injured man out of a shattered building in Wilhelmshaven. Many Germans survived the bombing only to be trapped beneath the mountains of rubble, where they suffocated.

Schutzraum 2
50 Personen
Ruhe bewahren!
Rauchen verboten!

Berliners wait out an air raid inside an underground shelter. A sign on the wall orders: "Keep Quiet! No Smoking!" A direct hit on the building above could cave in the structure, entombing everyone.

Salvaging Goods and Clearing Debris

Two twelve-year-old Hitler Youth members salvage wood from a bombed house in Berlin. Hoarded as a precious commodity, wood was used to make fires for cooking as well as to cover broken windows.

One of the groups of female
volunteers who became known
as Berlin's "rubble women"
clear debris from a bombed-out
building. By 1945, an estimated
400 million cubic meters of
rubble blanketed the Reich.

Their spirits intact despite the devastation, children in Cologne use a fallen building beam as a slide.

Pails in hand, Berliners line up
at a municipal fountain to draw
a day's supply of water for
washing and cooking. Bombs
frequently ruptured city mains,
cutting off water supplies for
large segments of the population.

After a big raid, Berliners gather
near the Brandenburg Gate to
scoop rations from cans of food
supplied by the government. One
city resident claimed that the
staples of her diet were ersatz
coffee, rolls, and "powdered eggs
diluted and stirred, scrambled,
and fried, and tasting of glue."

Lacking electricity and gas, Berlin women cook over coal-burning stoves set up in the street. The common ordeal brought neighbors closer together. "It was horrific, and I know it may sound foolish," a resident later admitted, "but people were never so friendly or so good again."

A couple in Hamburg hangs laundry to dry in an apartment stripped of its walls. Recalling an earlier Nazi promise to provide everyone with a healthful environment, one citizen joked: "Well, now we have all the sun and air we need!"

B. NITZSCHE

Zum Damen-u. Herrer

Surrounded by her belongings, an elderly woman takes a meager meal beneath a statue in the Hamburg suburb of Altona. After ten straight days of bombing in 1943, two-thirds of Hamburg's 1.5 million residents evacuated the city.

A family escapes from Hamburg carrying a few possessions in a wooden cart. A woman living in an outlying town later noted that the traumatized refugees refused to stop even when offered food and drink: "All they wanted to do was get away."

Victims of a December 1944 raid cover the floor of a Berlin gymnasium that has been incongruously decorated with Christmas trees.

An old woman in search of a loved one stares bleakly at a pile of bodies, her face set in quiet despair. More than 77,000 civilians were never found after the bombings.

Acknowledgments

The editors thank the following individuals and institutions for their help in the preparation of this book: France: Fort d'Ivry—Alain Alexandra and Patrick Bouhet, Documentaliste-Historien, DCEA. Germany: Berlin—Andreas Engelhardt, Zentralbild; Heidi Klein, Bildarchiv Preussischer Kulturbesitz; Wolfgang Streubel, Ullstein Bilderdienst. Koblenz—Meinrad Nilges, Bundesarchiv. Munich—Elisabeth Heidt, Süddeutscher Verlag Bilderdienst; Robert Hoffmann. Osnabrück—Karl-Walter Becker. Stuttgart—Manfred Rommel, Lord Mayor. United States: Washington, D.C.—Charles V.P. von Luttichau.

Picture Credits

Credits from left to right are separated by semicolons; from top to bottom by dashes.

Cover: Bundesarchiv, Koblenz. 4, 5: Ullstein Bilderdienst, Berlin. 6: Süddeutscher Verlag Bilderdienst, Munich. 8, 9: Map by R. R. Donnelley & Sons Company, Cartographic Services. 13: Bundesarchiv, Koblenz. 14: Ullstein Bilderdienst, Berlin. 15: Keystone, Paris—Ullstein Bilderdienst, Berlin. 16, 17: Bildarchiv Preussischer Kulturbesitz, Berlin; Süddeutscher Verlag Bilderdienst, Munich. 19, 22: Bundesarchiv, Koblenz. 25: The Hulton Picture Company, London. 26, 27: Archives Tallandier, Paris. 28, 29: Presse-illustrationen Heinrich R. Hoffmann, Munich. 30, 31: Robert Capa/Magnum, New York; Archives Tallandier, Paris. 32: DND/National Archives of Canada/PA-128792, Ottawa. 33: Bildarchiv Preussischer Kulturbesitz, Berlin. 34: Bundesarchiv, Koblenz. 36: S.I.R.P.A./E.C.P. Armées, Paris. 38, 39: Ullstein Bilderdienst, Berlin. 40-45: Background, Bundesarchiv, Koblenz, insets Erwin Bohm, courtesy Manfred Rommel (5). 46: Süddeutscher Verlag Bilderdienst, Munich. 49: Ullstein Bilderdienst, Berlin. 50: Bundesarchiv, Koblenz. 51: From *Mémorial Album Normandie*, Editions Heimdal, Bayeux, 1983, Corina. 52, 53: From *Mémorial Album Normandie*, Editions Heimdal, Bayeux, 1983, Corina; Roger-Viollet, Paris. 55: R. James Bender Publications, San Jose, California. 56: From *Mémorial Album Normandie*, Editions Heimdal, Bayeux, 1983, Bundesarchiv, Koblenz. 57: Bildarchiv Preussischer Kulturbesitz, Berlin. 58: From *Mémorial Album Normandie*, Editions Heimdal, Bayeux, 1983, Bundesarchiv, Koblenz. 60, 61: Archiv für Kunst und Geschichte, Berlin. 64: Ullstein Bilderdienst, Berlin. 65: Archives Tallandier, Paris. 66, 67: Ullstein Bilderdienst, Berlin. 68, 69: J. P. Benamou, copied from *Mémorial Album Normandie*, Editions Heimdal, Bayeux, 1983. 70: Map by R. R. Donnelley & Sons Company, Cartographic Services. 73: Archives Tallandier, Paris. 74: J. P. Benamou, copied from *Mémorial Album Normandie*, Editions Heimdal, Bayeux, 1983. 76, 77: Georges Bernage, copied from *Album Mémorial, Bataille de Caen*, Editions Heimdal, Bayeux, 1988 (2); Imperial War Museum, copied from *Panzers in Normandy Then and Now*, by Eric Lefèvre, Great Britain, 1983. 79: Süddeutscher Verlag Bilderdienst, Munich. 80: Bundesarchiv, Koblenz. 83: Ullstein Bilderdienst, Berlin. 84: Süddeutscher Verlag Bilderdienst, Munich. 85: U. S. Army, copied from *Mémorial Album Normandie*, Editions Heimdal, Bayeux, 1983. 86: The Bettmann Archive, New York. 87: Courtesy Editions Heimdal, Bayeux, Bundesarchiv, Koblenz. 90: AP/Wide World, New York. 91: Bundesarchiv, Koblenz. 92: Süddeutscher Verlag Bilderdienst, Munich—from *Die Leibstandarte im Bild*, by Rudolf Lehmann, Munin Verlag Osnabrück, 1983. 93: Brian Davis Collection, South Croydon, Surrey. 95: Map by R. R. Donnelley & Sons Company, Cartographic Services. 97: Bundesarchiv, Koblenz. 98: S.I.R.P.A./E.C.P. Armées, Paris—Bundesarchiv, Koblenz. 99: H. Furbringer, copied from *Mémorial Album Normandie*, Editions Heimdal, Bayeux, 1983—J. P. Benamou, courtesy Editions Heimdal, Bayeux. 101-103: Camera Press, London. 105: U. S. Army, copied from *La bataille de Provence 1943-1944*, courtesy Editions Charles-Lavauzelle, Paris, 1984. 106, 107: S.I.R.P.A./E.C.P. Armées, Paris. 108, 109: Archives Tallandier, Paris. 110, 111: The Bettmann Archive, New York. 112, 113: Ullstein Bilderdienst, Berlin; Edimedia, Paris. 114: S.I.R.P.A./E.C.P. Armées, Paris. 115: Photo Pichonnier, Paris. 116, 117: The Bettmann Archive, New York; Roger-Viollet, Paris. 118, 119: Imperial War Museum, London. 120, 121: Imperial War Museum, London; photo by H. Josse, courtesy Musée des collections historiques de la préfecture de police. 122: Bildarchiv Preussischer Kulturbesitz, Berlin. 124, 125: Erich Andres, Hamburg. 127: Süddeutscher Verlag Bilderdienst, Munich. 130, 131: Süddeutscher Verlag Bilderdienst, Munich (2)—Werner Held, Ransbach. 132, 133: Smithsonian Institution B23415. 134, 135: Werner Held, Ransbach. 136-139: Süddeutscher Verlag Bilderdienst, Munich. 141: Bildarchiv Preussischer Kulturbesitz, Berlin. 142, 143: Presseillustrationen Heinrich R. Hoffmann, Munich. 144, 145: Artwork by John Batchelor. 147: Werner Held, Ransbach. 148, 149: Süddeutscher Verlag Bilderdienst, Munich; Smithsonian Institution 60033AC. 150: Smithsonian Institution 53288AC. 151: Imperial War Museum, London. 153: Bildarchiv Preussischer Kulturbesitz, Berlin. 154, 155: Imperial War Museum, London. 156, 157: Süddeutscher Verlag Bilderdienst, Munich; Erich Andres, Hamburg—Süddeutscher Verlag Bilderdienst, Munich. 158, 159: Süddeutscher Verlag Bilderdienst, Munich; Imperial War Museum, London. 160, 161: Fischer-Foto, Erftstadt-Niederberg. 162, 163: FPG International, New York—International News Photo/The Bettmann Archive, New York; Süddeutscher Verlag Bilderdienst, Munich. 164, 165: Globe Photos, New York; Erich Andres, Hamburg (2). 166, 167: Imperial War Museum, London; Bildarchiv Preussischer Kulturbesitz, Berlin.

Bibliography

Books

Air Historical Group, *Europe* (Vol. 2 of *The Army Air Forces in World War II*). Ed. by Wesley Frank Craven and James Lea Cate. Chicago: University of Chicago Press, 1949.

Bailey, Ronald H., and the Editors of Time-Life Books, *The Air War in Europe* (World War II series). Alexandria, Va.: Time-Life Books, 1981.

Balfour, Michael, *Withstanding Hitler in Germany, 1933-45*. London: Routledge, 1988.

Beck, Earl R., *Under the Bombs*. Lexington: University Press of Kentucky, 1986.

Bernage, Georges, comp:
Bataille de Caen. Bayeux, France: Editions Heimdal, 1988.
Normandie Album Memorial. Transl. by Philippe Jutras. Bayeux, France: Editions Heimdal, 1983.

Blumenson, Martin, *Breakout and Pursuit*. Washington, D.C.: Office of the Chief of Military History, United States Army, 1961.

Blumenson, Martin, and the Editors of Time-Life Books, *Liberation* (World War II series). Alexandria, Va.: Time-Life Books, 1978.

Botting, Douglas, and the Editors of Time-Life Books, *The Second Front* (World War II series). Alexandria, Va.: Time-Life Books, 1978.

Brett-Smith, Richard, *Hitler's Generals*. San Rafael, Calif.: Presidio Press, 1976.

Buell, Thomas B., et al., *The Second World War*. Wayne, N.J.: Avery, 1984.

Carell, Paul, *Invasion—They're Coming!* Transl. by E. Osers. New York: E. P. Dutton, 1963.

Cave Brown, Anthony, *Bodyguard of Lies*. New York: Harper & Row, 1975.

Charman, Terry, *The German Home Front, 1939-45*. London: Barrie & Jenkins, 1989.

Choltitz, Dietrich von, *Brennt Paris? Adolf Hitler*. Mannheim, Germany: UNA Weltbücherei, 1950.

Collins, Larry, and Dominique Lapierre, *Is Paris Burning?* New York: Simon and Schuster, 1965.

Desquesnes, Rémy, *Le Mur de l'Atlantique en Normandie*. Bayeux, France: Editions Heimdal, 1976.

D'Este, Carlo, *Decision in Normandy*. New York: E. P. Dutton, 1983.

Eisenhower, David, *Eisenhower*. New York: Random House, 1986.

Ellis, L. F., *The Battle of Normandy* (Vol. 1 of *Victory in the West*). London: Her Majesty's Stationery Office, 1962.

Ethell, Jeffrey, and Alfred Price, *The German Jets in Combat*. London: Jane's, 1979.

Fey, Will, *Armor Battles of the Waffen-SS, 1943-45*. Transl. by Harri Henschler.

Winnipeg, Manitoba: J. J. Fedorowicz, 1990.

Florentin, Eddy, *The Battle of the Falaise Gap*. Transl. by Mervyn Savill. New York: Hawthorn Books, 1965.

Gaujac, Paul, *La bataille de Provence, 1943-1944*. Paris: Charles-Lavauzelle, 1984.

Giles, Geoffrey J., *Students and National Socialism in Germany*. Princeton, N.J.: Princeton University Press, 1985.

Harrison, Gordon A., *Cross-Channel Attack*. Washington, D.C.: Office of the Chief of Military History, United States Army, 1951.

Hastings, Max, *Overlord*. New York: Simon and Schuster, 1984.

Held, Werner, and Holger Nauroth, *The Defense of the Reich*. Transl. by David Roberts. New York: Arco, 1982.

Irving, David, *The Trail of the Fox*. New York: E. P. Dutton, 1977.

Kardorff, Ursula von, *Diary of a Nightmare*. Transl. by Ewan Butler. New York: John Day, 1966.

Keegan, John:
The Second World War. New York: Viking, 1989.
Six Armies in Normandy. New York: Viking Press, 1982.

Koch, H. W., *The Hitler Youth*. New York: Dorset Press, 1975.

Law, Richard D., and Craig W. H. Luther, *Rommel*. San Jose, Calif.: R. James Bender, 1980.

Lefèvre, Eric, *Panzers in Normandy*. London: Battle of Britain Prints, 1983.

Lewin, Ronald, *Rommel as Military Commander*. London: B. T. Batsford, 1968.

Liddell Hart, B. H., *History of the Second World War*. New York: G. P. Putnam's Sons, 1971.

Littlejohn, David, *The Hitler Youth*. Alexandria, Va.: Johnson Reference Books, 1988.

The Luftwaffe, by the Editors of Time-Life Books (The Epic of Flight series). Alexandria, Va.: Time-Life Books, 1982.

Majdalany, Fred, *The Fall of Fortress Europe*. Garden City, N.Y.: Doubleday, 1968.

Meyer, Hubert, *Kriegsgeschichte der 12.SS-Panzerdivision "Hitlerjugend"* (Vol. 2). Osnabrück: Munin Verlag, 1982.

Middlebrook, Martin:
The Battle of Hamburg. New York: Charles Scribner's Sons, 1981.
The Nuremberg Raid, 30-31 March 1944. New York: William Morrow, 1974.

Mitcham, Samuel W., Jr.:
Hitler's Legions. New York: Dorset Press, 1985.
Rommel's Last Battle. New York: Stein and Day, 1983.

Munson, Kenneth, *German War Birds from*

World War I to NATO Ally. New York: New Orchard Editions, 1986.

Murray, Williamson, *Strategy for Defeat*. Secaucus, N.J.: Chartwell Books, 1986.

Norman, Albert, *Operation Overlord*. Westport, Conn.: Greenwood Press, 1952.

Perrett, Bryan, *The PzKpfw V Panther*. London: Osprey, 1981.

Price, Alfred, *Luftwaffe*. New York: Ballantine Books, 1969.

Robichon, Jacques, *The Second D-Day*. Transl. by Barbara Shuey. New York: Walker, 1962.

Rommel, Erwin, *The Rommel Papers*. Ed. by B. H. Liddell Hart, transl. by Paul Findlay. New York: Da Capo Press, 1953.

Ruge, Friedrich, *Rommel in Normandy*. Transl. by Ursula R. Moessner. San Rafael, Calif.: Presidio Press, 1979.

Ryan, Cornelius, *The Longest Day*. New York: Simon and Schuster, 1959.

Saunders, Hilary St. George, *The Fight is Won* (Vol. 3 of *Royal Air Force, 1939-1945*). London: Her Majesty's Stationery Office, 1975.

Scholl, Inge, *Students against Tyranny*. Transl. by Arthur R. Schultz. Middletown, Conn.: Wesleyan University Press, 1970.

Seaton, Albert, *The Fall of Fortress Europe, 1943-1945*. New York: Holmes & Meier, 1981.

Shirer, William L., *The Rise and Fall of the Third Reich*. New York: Simon and Schuster, 1960.

Speidel, Hans, *Invasion 1944*. Westport, Conn.: Greenwood Press, 1971.

Strawson, John, *Hitler's Battles for Europe*. New York: Charles Scribner's Sons, 1971.

Thornton, Willis, *The Liberation of Paris*. New York: Harcourt, Brace & World, 1962.

Weigley, Russell F., *Eisenhower's Lieutenants*. Bloomington: Indiana University Press, 1981.

Werth, Alexander, *The Last Days of Paris*. London: Hamish Hamilton, 1940.

Whiting, Charles, and the Editors of Time-Life Books, *The Home Front: Germany* (World War II series). Alexandria, Va.: Time-Life Books, 1982.

Willmott, H. P., *June 1944*. Dorset: Blandford Press, 1984.

Wilmot, Chester, *The Struggle for Europe*. New York: Harper & Brothers, 1952.

Wilt, Alan F.:
The Atlantic Wall. Ames: Iowa State University Press, 1975.
The French Riviera Campaign of August 1944. Carbondale: Southern Illinois University Press, 1981.

Young, Desmond, *Rommel*. New York: William Morrow, 1950.

Young, Richard Anthony, *The Flying Bomb*. London: Ian Allan, 1978.

Index